Herbert Tuttle

German political Leaders

Herbert Tuttle

German political Leaders

ISBN/EAN: 9783743321663

Manufactured in Europe, USA, Canada, Australia, Japa

Cover: Foto ©ninafisch / pixelio.de

Manufactured and distributed by brebook publishing software (www.brebook.com)

Herbert Tuttle

German political Leaders

BRIEF BIOGRAPHIES

GERMAN
POLITICAL LEADERS

BY

HERBERT TUTTLE

NEW YORK
G. P. PUTNAM'S SONS
182 FIFTH AVENUE
1880

EDITOR'S PREFACE.

THE author of this volume is already well known to many Americans through his letters from Berlin to the New York *Tribune*, and to the London *Daily News*, as well by his Essays on German themes, in the *Gentleman's Magazine*, and elsewhere. Being a native of the United States, and a four years' resident of Berlin, he is remarkably well situated for the preparation of this particular book; as he may be supposed to understand both his subject and his audience. Our best books of reference afford such scanty information in respect to German statesmen, that a work like this cannot fail to possess great popular value.

T. W. H.

NEWPORT, R. I., April 3, 1876.

PREFACE.

THE larger portion of the men described in this volume will, doubtless, be here introduced to American readers for the first time. So overshadowing are the fame and authority of Prince Bismarck, so recent was the introduction, and so crude is the present state of parliamentary life in Germany, that the minor personages, who are concerned with the modest and obscure details of the system, are but little known abroad. This is a misfortune, and, also, a mistake. I am firmly convinced that the experiment which Germany is making in constitutional government, is already rich in lessons for the philosophic student of politics, and ought not to be neglected, even by the most hurried observer of current events. The preparation of this book has, therefore, been an agreeable duty. Biography is often more attractive than history; and I have taken advantage of this fact, to insinuate, now and then, upon the unsuspecting reader general facts and deductions, from which he might otherwise have escaped. But the history of the early constitutional struggles in Prussia and Germany has yet to be written.

Some of the gentlemen included in the following pages are personally known to me, and the careers of all of them have been critically observed during an uninterrupted residence of nearly four years in Germany. I have not scrupled, therefore, to reproduce a few passages from earlier contributions of my own to the daily and other periodical press. All extracts from foreign sources, on the other hand, have been specifically acknowledged.

H. T.

BERLIN, March, 1876.

CONTENTS.

I.—THE CHANCELLOR.

	PAGE
1. Prince Bismarck	1

II.—MINISTERS.

2. Dr. Falk	25
3. President Delbrück	39
4. Herr Camphausen	49

III.—THE DIPLOMATIC SERVICE.

5. Prince Hohenlohe	61
6. Count von Arnim	73

IV.—THE PARLIAMENTARIANS.

7. Herr von Bennigsen	91
8. Dr. Simson	101

V.—THE PARTY LEADERS.

9. Herr Lasker	113
10. Herr Windthorst	129
11. Dr. Loewe	139
12. Herr Schulze-Delitzsch	148
13. Herr Jacoby	160
14. Herr Hasselmann	176
15. Herr Sonnemann	192

VI.—THE SCHOLARS IN POLITICS.

16. Professor Gneist	203
17. Professor Virchow	216
18. Professor Treitschke	233
19. Professor von Sybel	247

PART I.

THE CHANCELLOR.

I.

PRINCE BISMARCK.

THE historians have a theory which derives the family name, Bismarck, from "Bischoffs-Marck," or "Bishop's Limits," from a domain that was once ceded by the Bishop of Havelberg to the ancestors of the great Prussian. The family came from Stendal, a town about sixty miles from Berlin, where they are traced back to the fourteenth century. One Rule von Bismarck appears in the records of these turbulent times to have played an important part in the guild of tailors and in the town council, and to have been excommunicated in consequence of disputes with the clergy, as to the management of the town schools. His son, Claus, leader of the aristocracy, was banished by the Democratic party. Among these earlier representatives, as well as among their descendants, we find several who distinguished themselves both in military and political service. In the early part of this century, the house was represented by Carl Wilhelm Ferdinand von Bismarck, who is described as a "noble, genial, kind-hearted man," a retired soldier, who rose to the rank of Captain of cavalry. His wife, whom he married in 1806, was a Fräulein Menken, a refined and cultivated woman. They lived at Schönhausen, a roomy estate near Stendal, which the family had acquired ; and here, on the 1st of April, 1815, Otto Edward Leopold, the fourth child, was born.

Herr Görlach, in his excellent little biography of the Prince, describes him as a youth of a very tender nature. In his sixth year, while his family were living on the Kniephof estate in Pomerania, Otto "was sent to an educational institute at Berlin, where the extreme severity of the treatment wounded the boy's soft nature. He had found his brother Bernhard there, but still he suffered greatly from home-sickness, and could not watch the ploughmen ploughing in the fields without tears. The two boys passed from one Berlin school to another, according to their progress and ages ; and later, when they were living in their father's house in Berlin, the direction of their studies was confided to private tutors."

His tutor describes him at this period as quick of apprehension, industrious, with a good memory, and fond of the history of his own country. As a Protestant he was a pupil of and was confirmed by the great theologian and pulpit orator, Schleiermacher.

From the private tutor he passed, in 1832, to the University of Göttingen. At this place the "tenderness" of his nature seems to have deserted him, as well as his earlier habits of study, for he was a leader in all the most characteristic sports and excesses of German student-life. He was a species of college champion, the best boxer and fencer, drinker, and rider. Of his studies there, it is enough to say that one professor declares he never saw him at his lectures. From a multitude of reminiscences out of the period of Bismarck's life I select one which he himself has very lately furnished. The publisher of the *Public Ledger* in Philadelphia, sent the Prince at Varzin a cane made from the wood of Independence Hall; and in acknowledgment of the gift received the following interesting letter :

"VARZIN, JULY 4, 1875.

"DEAR SIR :—You have had the goodness to send me, as a support for my old days, a cane made from the tower from whose heights, ninety-nine years ago, the bell was rung for the first time in honor of that great commonwealth, whose ship bells now sound their full and welcome tongues in all harbors of the world. For this historical treasure I beg you to accept my heartiest thanks. I shall honor it, carefully preserve it, and, with other relics of remarkable years, bequeath it to my children. This day is one of those which always recall to my mind the happy hours that I have spent on many a fourth of July, with American friends, the first time with John Lothrop Motley, Mitchell G. King, and Amory Coffin, in 1832, at Göttingen. I only wish that you, my dear sir, and I could always be as sound and happy as we four lusty fellows, when forty-three years ago we celebrated the Fourth of July at Göttingen. VON BISMARCK."

These little glimpses into his early life and character might be supplemented by an extract from a letter to his favorite sister, "Maldewine," and to his wife. To the latter he writes on one occasion : "The day before yesterday

I went to Wiesbaden, and looked with a mixture of sadness and premature wisdom at the scenes of my former follies. If only it would please God to fill up with clear strong wine the vessel in which at twenty-one the muddy champagne of youth frothed up to so little purpose! . . . How many of those with whom I flirted and drank and gambled are now underground! What changes my views of life have undergone in the fourteen years that have elapsed since that time, each in its turn seeming to me the correct one; how much that I then thought great now appears small; how much now seems honorable which I then despised! How much fresh foliage may still grow out of our inner man, giving shade, rustling in the wind, becoming worthless and faded, before another fourteen years are passed, before 1865, if only we live so long! I cannot imagine how a man who thinks at all about himself, and yet refuses to hear anything about God, can endure life without weariness and self-abhorrence."

On the occasion of the death of his sister's child, ten years later, he writes a letter of consolation, full of the most tender Christian sentiments, and even in the stormy period of 1864, he closes a political letter to a friend with the following confession of faith: "You see from this that I take a common-sense view of the question; besides, my feeling of gratitude for the support which God has given us rises into the conviction that He also knows how to turn our errors into our good; I feel this daily and am at once humiliated and comforted."

His domestic tastes were always strong, and find expression in the entire course of his correspondence. His longing for a wife and household of his own would seem to have been very acute, till in 1847, it was satisfied by his marriage with Johanna von Putkammer. Three children—Marie, born in 1848, Herbert in 1849, William in 1852—are the fruit of this union.

We return now to trace the steps in his professional course. After leaving Göttingen, he attended some lectures at Berlin, and in 1835 was qualified as *Auscultator*, the first degree in a German advocate's career. In the winter of this year he was presented at court, and met, for the first time, his present sovereign and master, then Prince William of Prussia. In 1836, he was admitted to the service of the Government, and was assigned to duty at Aix-la-Chapelle—a position that gave him much intercourse with foreigners, and was of great influence in shaping his future political character. A little later he was transferred to the district of Potsdam, where he served his year in the army. In 1839, the death of his mother and illness of his father recalled him to the family estates in Pomerania, of which he and his brother assumed the management, a relation which lasted till 1845, and threatened for ever to put an end to his political career. But in that year his father died, and the property was divided. The estate of Schönhausen fell to the share of Otto, and the term has ever since formed an integral part of his name. The next two years were those of a country gentleman, farming, shooting, riding, with a little local politics, and finally, in 1847, an election to the Assembly of the Estates or United Diet of February. With this event ends one period and begins another of Bismarck's life.

In this year the political fermentation in Prussia had reached a crisis. The broken pledges of Frederic William III., to give his people a written constitution, had been renewed by his successor, Frederic William IV., and their fulfilment delayed in the same manner. The concession of the United Diet of 1847, was only wrung from him by the irresistible necessities of the time. Even then it was a concession in form from which the spirit revolted, for in the throne speech at the opening of the deliberation, the king declared that no power on earth should ever succeed in moving him to transform the natural relation between Sovereign and People into a conventional, constitutional one; and never would he consent that a written document should be allowed to intrude between the Lord God in Heaven and his country and to take the place of the ancient faith. These were unpromising ideas on which to base a scheme of constitutional reform, and all patriots foresaw stormy times. But the King was not without stalwart friends. The old country *Junkers* rallied generally around his most arbitrary maxims, and none more heartily than Herr Otto von Bismarck.

One or two speeches will give a rough idea of his views of this period. His first appearance in the tribune was on the 17th of May; the occasion was to correct what he regarded as a false theory of the uprising in 1813 to expel the French. A deputy had pretended that the people came to the relief of their King because he had promised them a written constitution. Bismarck protested that this view was not only false but dishonorable. The people of Prussia, he declared, did not rise to throw off the yoke of domestic but of foreign servitude. He did not shrink from the title of *Junker*. "I am proud of being a Prussian *Junker*," said he once, "and feel myself honored by the name." Again, in June of the same year, he said, "The only question is, who has the right to give an authentic and legally-binding interpretation of a doubtful law? In my opinion, no one but the King; and this conviction lies, as I believe, in the popular sense of right. It is difficult to get at the opinion of the people; in some of the places in the central provinces I think I have discovered it, and have found it to be still the old popular Prussian belief, that the word of a King is more than all the turning and twisting of the letter of the law."

This is indeed the opinion of an extreme conservative, but of one who did not despise reason and reasoning. English examples were constantly cited, and to these Bismarck invariably replied: "Give us everything English that we have not got; give us the English fear of God, English respect for laws, the entire English constitution, but also the exact circumstances of the English land-owner —English riches, and English public spirit,—then we shall be able to govern as they do."

The first united *Landtag* gave way to the second, and this in time to the constituent Parliament; the insurrection of March, after a few angry spurts, had everywhere succumbed to the Prussian military; and the result was a frightened and obstinate King surrounded by a band of faithful followers, and an assembly in which a fierce and determined radicalism held control.

In these preliminary conflicts Herr von Bismarck had shown a determined zeal for the integrity of the Prussian crown, and withal such a generous sympathy with the Austrian element in German politics, that on the assembling of the Frankfort Diet in 1851, he was attached to the Prussian delegation as Councilor and Secretary. One of his letters from that city gives an amusing sketch of the method of diplomacy as then, at least, practiced.

"I am making tremendous progress," he writes, "in the art of saying absolutely nothing in a great many words. I write sheets of reports which read quite well and fluently, like leading articles, but if Manteuffel [then President of the Ministry], when he has read them, can say what they contain, he is cleverer than I am. Each one behaves as if he believed that the other were crammed full of ideas and plans, if he would only tell them; and, meanwhile, not one of us is an atom the wiser as to what will become of Germany. Nobody, not even the most evil-minded skeptic of a Democrat, would believe what an amount of charlatanry and bragging there is in diplomacy."

Later, the same year, he was appointed Ambassador at the Diet, and gradually became, instead of a friend, a most energetic foe of Austrian policy. This position he retained till 1859, when he was transferred to St. Petersburg. During this period he had not only obtained a deep practical insight into the German system, or want of system; but he had made many useful and pleasant visits to different countries. He traveled in Holland, Belgium, Denmark, and Sweden, and he was twice in Paris, in 1855 and 1857. The second time he had a long conversation with the Emperor Napoleon. His appointment to the Russian Court he owed to the partiality of Prince William, who became Regent in 1858.

In 1861, on the death of Frederic William IV., the Prince Regent became King; and soon afterward, as is understood, he formed the plan of making his Ambassador on the Neva, Minister President of Prussia. In the meantime he served a few months at Paris, and entered the Ministry as Premier and Minister of Foreign Affairs on the 8th of October, 1862. The real warfare of his life began at this time. King and Minister had a perfect understanding about the policy to pursue. The King was a soldier and had the sympathy of Bismarck and the assistance of Roon and Moltke in the scheme of military reform, to which he at once began to devote himself. The Minister had resolved on the expulsion of Austria as the condition of a strong and enduring Germany. The details of these two independent schemes—pursued in the face of an unwilling people and in spite of Legislatures which had the constitutional right to defeat them—make up one of the most exciting and instructive epochs in modern history. The government could not reveal its ultimate plans without ruining them; and it had too much contempt for democracy to respect even the forms of Parliamentary institutions. The House was overwhelmingly Liberal; it hated Bismarck and distrusted the King; and to strengthen the army seemed but to strengthen its own fetters. It refused the appropriation, and the Ministry steadily made them on its own responsibility. Again and again the House was dissolved; new elections only added to the majority of the opposition.

The Danish war in 1864 did not give pause to the Liberals. As men, they felt for provinces which had provoked the rapacity of two great powers; as patriots, they saw but little glory in such a victory of the national arms. The struggle was continued with fresh bitterness. All the efforts of Bismarck at this time were toward the final conflict with Austria. In the diplomatic struggle at Frankfort his aim throughout was not only to assert the rights of Prussia in the confederation against the annoyance of Austria, but also to detach from the latter the sympathy and support of the smaller German States. By enticing Austria into a separate alliance with Prussia for the conquest of Schleswig, he shook or hoped to shake the confidence of the smaller States in their Danubian ally. In regard to internal reforms he even outbid his rival. The Austrian Ministry, in order to prolong their supremacy in the confederation, offered to establish a Congress of delegates from the different States. Prussia, through her Minister, took the almost revolutionary step of proposing an elective national parliament. The conquest and joint occupation of the Duchies was a measure that puzzled everybody. It was made in the face of three great hostile powers, England and Russia, which were connected by marriage, and France, which was connected by political sympathy with Denmark, and against the opposition of all Liberals, who saw in this alliance of the two leading German States the disappearance of all hopes for a Liberal, united Germany. This is perhaps the period in which Bismarck's sagacity and firmness as a statesman were most severely tried.

His views at the time are clearly stated in the following dispatch to the smaller German courts, dated March 24th, 1866:

"The interests of Prussia and of Germany," he says, "are identical from their geographical position. This matter concerns our advantage as well as that of Germany. If we are not sure of Germany, then our situation will be more endangered than that of the other European States;

but the fate of Prussia will draw that of Germany after it, and we do not doubt that, if her power were once broken, Germany would only retain a passive share in European politics. The German Governments ought all to consider it a sacred duty to guard against this, and therefore to unite with Prussia."

This reasoning was lost on the Southern powers. When the conflict finally came, and Prussia and Austria met at Sadowa, nearly all the petty German princes fought and lost with the latter.

The peace of Prague gave the conquered provinces of Schleswig to Prussia, as well as Hanover, Hesse-Cassel, Nassau, and the free City of Frankfort on the Main. The North German Confederation, which was formed on the ruins of the old confederation, included Prussia, the States and free cities of the Baltic Coast, and Saxony, Saxe-Weimar, Brunswick, Saxe-Coburg-Gotha, and Anhalt, while the remaining States organized the South German Confederation. By the same peace, Italy, the ally of Prussia, recovered Venice from Austria; while the Emperor Napoleon, who had been trying to obtain—first from Prussia, then from Austria—a share of the spoil, was a helpless spectator of events.

The interval from the Austrian war to the French war—from 1866 to 1870—was one, for the most, of peaceful legislative reform. Domestic affairs received the most attention, just as foreign affairs had done before that period. These, of course, exacted of a statesman a different class of qualities. There is a school of critics who pretend that Bismarck, though a bold and astute diplomatist, fitted to cope with giants in international politics, is not adapted by nature or training for the more humble but equally important details of home legislation. This theory is worth a moment's examination.

I have already given in extracts from letters the reflections which the Frankfort Diet inspired in Herr von Bismarck. I have also mentioned his sweeping proposal, in 1866, to concede the German people a national representative parliament, as a means of satisfying the Democratic aspiration of the people, and of cementing the proposed German Union. When the constituent Parliament of the North German Confederation met, and not before, Bismarck, now become Count Bismarck, had an opportunity to try the experiment. The First National Parliament of Germany was called into being. The other great measure of unification was the re-establishment, with improved modifications, of the Zollverein. A common parliament and a common tariff were held to be the two chief pillars of unity. The latter institution, too, was extended to the South German States. Throughout this period Count Bismarck appeared to good advantage. He was in the prime of life, he had conquered his previous unpopularity, a good feeling subsisted between court, ministry, and majority, and the work of internal reform proceeded for the most part smoothly. The only sharp debates were over the relations of the North German States to the Northern Confederation; and here Bismarck was often forced to check the zeal of Liberals, who would have driven those States into an unwilling union. No man was more thoroughly and effectively a German, but he saw that, at some date, the force of circumstances would effect a more durable union than any act of legislation.

Prince Bismarck has gained such an extraordinary position in the field of diplomacy and general politics, that to his position as a leader in legislation is awarded a minor importance. But he would have won no insignificant rank even as a private and untitled member. A great orator, indeed, he is not, and would in no circumstances become. Not to mention other defects, he wants imagination, the power of pathos, real or counterfeit, grace or art of manner, an effective voice, and a ready utterance. Without these, or some of these qualities, oratory, even of the second rank, is impossible. But without accepting Earl Russell's theory, that eloquence has no influence on parliamentary leadership, it is easy to show from history that the two are by no means inseparable. Such qualities as fit one for power in an assembly, independently of eloquence, Prince Bismarck conspicuously possesses. He can persuade or command with equal skill and equal effect; but he is, moreover, a debater of no ordinary accomplishments. He has a resolution which wins respect, if not obedience, and which, with a little less-military imperiousness, would be wonderfully effective. He is witty and humorous above most of his countrymen. He is always concise and forcible. His delivery is somewhat slow and hesitating, so that his speeches read as well as they sound; but they may be studied as models of exact, logical language. His faculty of condensing a plan or a policy into an epigram is so well known, that I shall surely be pardoned for citing such phrases as: "The battles of this generation are to be fought out with iron and blood," or, "We shall not go to Canossa," which has been adopted into the popular heart. And, finally, Prince Bismarck has the valuable art of keeping silent when it is inexpedient to speak.

Of himself Bismarck once said: "I am no orator. . . . I am not capable of working upon your feelings or obscuring facts with a play of words. My speech is simple and clear."

The following description is more just:

"There is no charm of speech, no fullness of expression in him, nothing to carry away the hearer. His voice, though clear and intelligible, is dry and unattractive, and its tone is monotonous. He interrupts himself; comes to a standstill, and sometimes almost stammers, as if his refractory tongue refused obedience, and he had to struggle painfully for the right way of expressing his thoughts; his restless movements backwards and forwards do not at all add to the impression produced by his words. But the longer he speaks, the more he overcomes all difficulties; he succeeds in fitting his words to his thoughts in the closest manner, and ends by throwing out powerful invectives, which, as we know, are often too powerful."

It does not fall within the province of the writer to pass judgment on the dispute between Prussia and France, nor do our limits allow even a recapitulation of the leading events. That a war with France had always been regarded by Bismarck as an inevitable condition of the future German Empire may confidently be affirmed, as well as that his foreign policy had steadily kept that fact in view. Beyond that, statesmanship retired before the army. When Bismarck had become assured of the fidelity of his South German allies, of the non-intervention of Russia, and of the impotence of Austria, England, and Italy, he was ready for the war. The course of events was marvelously in accordance with his previous plans.

Bismarck accompanied the army throughout the war until the final capitulation at Versailles. The direction of military affairs he left wholly to the soldiers, and took an active part only in the settlement of political questions. He himself has given an account of a characteristic camp scene after the battle of Gravelotte, when he was sitting with the King on a ladder supported by a barrel and a horse's carcass, composing the telegram with the news of the victory : " A telegraph official handed me his dispatch book, and then stood behind me, holding his horse. His Majesty dictated, I wrote. Thinking that a little *mousseux de Champagne* was advisable for the benefit of foreign countries, I had allowed myself to add a few embellishments to the telegram. But the modesty of our Royal Master, who always holds sternly to the plainest truth, would not tolerate this. In a second telegram the result of the victory was reduced to the barest limits. Then Moltke interfered, and also Roon, because certain errors had slipped into the military estimates. At last the fourth telegram was correct, and the official dashed off to the office with it."

He has also left accounts of the capitulation of Sedan, which have a biographical as well as an historical value. The crowning event of his life, the proclamation of the German Empire at Versailles, on the 18th day of January, 1871, wanted no element of picturesque effect, of historical solemnity, or of political significance. The preliminary treaty of peace was ratified by the French Assembly on the 1st of March. On the 21st of the same month,

Count von Bismarck became Prince von Bismarck and Chancellor of the German Empire.

The French war, like the Austrian, introduced a new order of things, to which it was necessary to adjust the civil and political machinery; and it has been followed by a course of domestic legislation extending to the present time. Most of this could have but little interest for foreign observers. On the 21st of March, 1871, the First Imperial Parliament of Germany—*Deutscher Reichstag*—met in Berlin, and was opened by the Emperor in person. The new Constitution was proclaimed on the 16th of April. In the fall of 1872, in consequence of ill-health and dissatisfaction with the adjustment of works, Prince Bismarck resigned the presidency of the Prussian cabinet, which was temporarily assigned to the Minister of War, Roon. The next spring, Roon retired from political life and Bismarck resumed his old place, with a vice-president to relieve him of routine work. In the winter of 1874, again, he sent in his resignation on account of a partial defeat in the *Reichstag* over the new army bill. A compromise was effected, however, and the Prince remained at his post. The important, nay, indispensable character of his services to Germany was shown by the widespread consternation produced by the rumor of retirement. His enemies allege that his original infirmities of temper have been aggravated by age and prolonged power. It is certain that he is very impatient under opposition and defeat.

By far the most important enterprise in which this active statesman has engaged since the French war, is the campaign against the power of the Roman Catholic Church in Germany. While the result is still pending, it would be premature to write the history of that conflict. Enough, that the proclamation of infallibility and the re-organization of the German Empire so affected the relation between Pope and Kaiser, that in the opinion of Prince Bismarck, —which the Emperor and the great mass of liberal Germans share,—a new adjustment, which should secure the State greater freedom of action, and more ample means of self-defense, had become imperatively necessary. This was a mixed Prussian and Imperial movement; and both governments, always, of course, under Bismarck's guidance, have taken legislative steps in the premises. The issue, as we have said, is still open. Both parties are confident of final victory; but it cannot be questioned, that the undertaking on the part of the Chancellor was one of the most extreme danger, and was sure to encounter the most formidable obstacles.

The adoption of this policy threw Prince Bismarck into a closer alliance with his old foes the Liberals, though his measures of home reform, since 1866, had generally enjoyed the support of that faction. In these later years, the old extreme Conservatives have been his most bitter opponents. This vast revolution in Bismarck's political opinions—and one more vast than from the old *Junker* reactionists to the Prussian Liberals can hardly be imagined—is one of the facts in his later career that have most invited the inquiry of critics. He represents in himself, in fact, two distinct phases or stages of a political career, and is admired from two quite different points of departure. He is at once a Prussian statesman and a German, and his course in the former capacity is often irreconcilable with that in the latter. Where the latter begins, the former seems to end.

Where the old school of Prussians cease to celebrate and abandon him as a renegade, there the great German nation takes him up and makes him an Imperial hero. Even the *Kreuz Zeitung*, the ultra Conservative organ, eulogizes him up to Sadowa, up to the fatal hour in which, returning a patrician conqueror, like Coriolanus, he made the fatal compromise with the spirit of plebeian Liberalism. It is sure that it would have been better for him to have fallen on the plains of Bohemia. When it warns the admirers of the Chancellor to be discreet and moderate in their tributes, it means that the path of commendation is clear only to 1866, and after that loses itself rapidly in the wilderness. This being the case, it would seem that the converse must be true, and that the period hallowed by the Reactionists must be odious to Liberals. It is, of course, easy, by selecting isolated expressions, oral or written, from a man's history, to convict him of almost any shade of political or other doctrine; but the diligent collection and ingenious arrangement of such passages has never, perhaps, been regarded with favor by the better class of philosophers. The same holds true, of course, with regard to Prince Bismarck. To attempt to make him out a Liberal in disguise from 1862 to 1866, because in letters he now and then expresses no abhorrence of Parliaments, is hard work in the face of the events of that period. This line of treatment is not complimentary to the Prince himself. He himself has often publicly explained that since 1866, and gradually, changes in his political opinion have taken place, and he has gloried in this elasticity. He calls it adapting one's self to circumstances, and again a growth in wisdom and experience. This honorable flexibility, he has said, distinguishes him from his old Conservative friends —from Gerlach, for instance. If Bismarck was always a Liberal, so was Gerlach; or, on the other hand, if Bismarck has not changed since 1866, he is to-day an intolerant *Junker* like Gerlach. The biographical test applied to practical politics is always one of the most treacherous and least useful.

It is, too, a striking illustration of Prince Bismarck's change of party relations, that he has provoked not only the enmity, but the cowardly vengeance of two different political factions. Two attempts on his life have been made. The first was in 1866, on the 7th of March, by one Blind, an adopted son of the well-known philanthropist and radical, Carl Blind. One or two of the shots grazed the clothes of Bismarck; but he had the coolness to seize his assailant and deliver him over to the police, after which he walked home and took part in a dinner party which he had appointed. The second attempted assassination was in 1874, at Kissingen, in Bavaria, the villain, this time, being an Ultramontane fanatic, named Kullman. On this occasion, too, the Prince was but slightly bruised in the hand by the bullet that was aimed at his heart.

Prince Bismarck may be called the founder of Prussian diplomacy. At his advent that branch of the public service was chiefly in the hands of dull country gentlemen, who were unfitted as well for the daily routine as for the occasional adventure, which are both in their time demanded; and they fell now into the hands of Nicholas of Russia, now of Metternich. Goethe was by no means a political satirist, but he makes the Chancellor say, in the second part of "Faust," that the priests and the knights, Church and Army, are the two chief props of State. In a theory not essentially different from this the Prussian people were educated. Accordingly, the profession of diplomacy long held a low rank there. In so far as the opposition of the military class was the natural opposition of brave and straightforward men to a service which is too often associated with trickery and falsehood, the feeling was respectable. Unfortunately it did not end there, nor was this its true basis. It sprang out of the narrow contempt felt by all Prussian soldiers for civil occupations, and was stimulated by jealousy for a service which is becoming such a powerful and indispensable servant of the State. Bismarck himself first gave the example of an active diplomatist, and afterward, becoming Premier, he made his example the rule of the service. He cemented the Italian alliance and threw dust in the eyes of France, while the army was fighting in Bohemia ; he kept Russia firm and friendly, while the Second Empire was going down under the charge of Moltke's legions. The Prince himself once described modestly his own services in the late war. It was on the eve of a great victory, and men were flocking around to congratulate him. He said, "I know nothing about strategy or the science of war. Let Moltke and the army have the credit. But you have seen Bavarians to-day on the field. Well, the presence of the Bavarians and other South Germans here, fighting with you, and not on the other side, is my work."

The case of Bismarck has sometimes been cited against the value of professional training for politicians. He appeared so suddenly on the field of European events, and assumed at once such a commanding position, that many have treated him as a prodigy in whom inspiration might almost be assumed. The premises here are as false as the inference from them is pernicious. It is true that no amount of study will wholly supply the place of natural genius or talent, but it is true also that simple genius without training and discipline, is often credited with achievements that it never performs. Otto von Bismarck is one of the most distinct results of thorough political education. His whole career previous to entering the Prussian Ministry, was one of study and preparation. At the gymnasium he acquired control of the English and French languages; and throughout his career they have served him in many a diplomatic crisis. At the university, he was a profound and philosophical student of history, particularly that of his own country; and even to-day, in Parliamentary debates, he often astonishes his colleagues by his mastery of such details. While he was at Frankfort, his letters show that he prized the position chiefly for the experience and the valuable lessons that it afforded him. At St. Petersburg there is but one report of his behavior. He lived in frugal style and gave few entertainments, but devoted himself assiduously to study and inquiry, and even became quite a proficient in the Russian language. These occupations did not give him notoriety, but they were not quite profitless. When in 1862 he assumed the direction of Prussian affairs, he brought to the duties a ripe experience, a familiarity with the languages and habits and politics of other nations, the resources of a mind which had never ceased to acquire and assimilate useful knowledge, and habits of industry which have since astonished all Europe. This and nothing else is the secret inspiration of the great German statesman.

PART II.

THE MINISTERS.

II.

DR. FALK.

THE title prefixed to this gentleman's name is a scholastic, not a professional one. Nothing is more strange than the popular German regard for this distinction, except, perhaps, the capricious way in which it clings to some men till it becomes almost an inseparable part of their names, while with others it is and remains an alien intruder. Bismarck, for instance, is a Doctor of Philosophy *honoris causa*, and always figures as such in books of record, but "Dr. Bismarck" is unknown to the public. Forckenbeck, the present president of the *Reichstag*, is never mentioned with the "Doctor's" title; his predecessor, Simson, never without it. The rising young politician who stands at the head of the Ministry of Public Worship and Education, Herr Adalbert Falk, is one to whom it is always applied by universal public consent.

Measured by the duration of his actual political service, Dr. Falk is, indeed, very young. Since the winter of 1872, he has been a minister with an independent portfolio;

previous to that, he was a bureau official without the right of initiating measures. These distinctions in the official hierarchy are less rigid elsewhere than in Prussia, and much less so in the United States, for instance, where the caprice of favoritism may defy the rules of prescription; but in Prussia they are of the greatest consequence. The rule is that the bureaucrat lives and dies as such. Promotion for him is only within the bounds of his clerical domain, and only an exception lifts him out into the region of ministerial independence. It is no uncommon thing to read in the press of some veteran celebrating the fiftieth anniversary of his entry into the public service. Half a century in the life of such a man has consumed perhaps a barrel of ink, several tons of paper, and quills enough to thatch the roof of the royal castle. He has sworn allegiance to three kings and put tallow candles in his window for two or three successful wars. The revenues of the kingdom for a twelvemonth could not tempt his official integrity. Beginning at a tall desk and standing, he passes thence to a three legged stool; next, to a wooden chair; and finally to a chair with a cushion; and here he remains on a salary of two or three thousand thalers a year, till, in his declining days, he is retired on a modest pension. These are the men, and this is the system that make up the bureaucratic government of Prussia.

By superior ability or superior fortune, Adalbert Falk escaped from this career of routine. He was born in the year 1827 at Metschkau, in Silesia. His father, a clergyman and member of the provincial consistory, belonged to the Schleiermacher school of liberal theology; but on the arrival of an era of doctrinal reaction under the orthodox King, Frederic William IV., he fell into disfavor, and retired to a country parish. Like so many of the so-called "liberal theologians," the elder Falk did not, I believe, extend his liberalism into politics. The meager salary of a "Landpastor" did not prevent the son from pursuing the ordinary educational course of German youth. He studied first in the "Realschule" of Landeshut, then at a gymnasium in Breslau, and finally at the university of the latter city. This is one of the two Prussian universities that have a Catholic faculty in theology, side by side with the Protestant. In 1847, he began his legal career, which in Prussian usage is treated almost as a state charge ; in 1850, he became an assistant of the Public Prosecutor in Breslau ; in 1853, chief of this office at Lyck ; in 1861, he assumed the same functions before the *Kammergericht*, or Superior Court, with duties in the Ministry of Justice ; in 1862, Judge of the Court of Appeals at Glogau ; and in 1868, he was permanently assigned as Privy Councillor, or *Geheimerath*, to the Ministry of Justice. Bismarck was Premier, and the Minister of Justice, Dr. Leonhardt, was one of the first fruits of the new policy of preferring able plebeians to incapable nobles for public office.

It may be said in explanation of Dr. Falk's rapid rise in the official scale, that it was a time of reform and experiment, when inventive genius was prized. A fresh man and a practical lawyer was likely to be more fertile in ideas and suggestions than one whose brain had become inert from prolonged routine. The newly-annexed provinces exacted new conditions of the national jurisprudence, while the North German Confederation called for an entire system of imperial laws. In this work of codification and drafting Dr. Falk was one of the most efficient. But soon he was assigned to a task of quite a different character. The conflict with the Church had broken out; the Prussian Government determined on a course of repressive or defensive legislation; and, after casting his eyes about for the proper man, Bismarck fixed on Dr. Falk. From this point most of the political interest in this gentleman dates. In order, however, to understand the subject, a passing acquaintance is necessary with the order of events, which led to the retirement of Dr. Von Mühler from the "Cultus" Ministry, and to the vast change of policy that retirement in itself alone implied.

Up to the year 1817, there was in Prussia no Ministry of Public Worship and Education. Those subjects had been assigned to bureaus in the Ministry of the Interior and placed in charge of subordinate officials; but in 1817, the king created a special department and placed Baron Altenstein at the head of it. He was a faithful officer and a prudent statesman. Without any meddlesome theories on theology, he worked in a practical way for educational reform, and to him, as much as to any one man, Prussia is indebted for her common schools. The successors of Altenstein, among whom Eichhorn and Stahl were the most eminent, made themselves notorious, not to say odious, by their hostility to the cause of natural science, which they systematically repressed at the command of a dictatorial theology. Protestants though they were, they preferred the sublime dogmatism of the Roman Catholic Church to the daring results of physical investigation. Accordingly, the Catholics made grave advances along the whole line of social, educational, and political interests. Under Raumer, a nephew of the great historian, and Hollweg, things were no better. The Church, or the ecclesiastical element, wielded paramount authority in the public councils.

This brings us to the first Cabinet of Bismarck in 1862, and his Minister of Public Worship, Dr. Von Mühler. He is the last representative of the old spirit. A learned, austere, and conscientious man, he held the most exalted theories of ecclesiastical prerogative, of the claims of birth, of divine right; and the policy adopted toward the Church of Rome after the close of the French war, met his opposition from the first. He was the reluctant agent of resistance to two of the earlier and more flagrant offences of the Catholic clergy. He conducted for the government the correspondence with Dr. Krementz, the obstinate and disobedient bishop of Ermeland. He sanctioned the removal of the Catholic Chaplain General, whom the Pope, in violation of legal forms, had endowed with the rank and functions of a bishop. Farther than this Von Mühler could not go; and when he heard that general laws, covering all such cases as the above, were in preparation, he resigned his office and retired from public life. On the 22d of January, 1872, he was succeeded by Dr. Falk.

The new minister was welcomed by the *Provinzial Correspondenz*, a weekly organ of the government, in the following words: "This ministerial change is an expression of the necessity, recognized by the crown, that the power of the State in religion and educational affairs be wielded by a spirit which offers guaranties of complete independence and rectitude, as well as of the earnest purpose to vindicate both the inalienable rights of the State, and the just claims of moral and spiritual interests." This was by no means a revolutionary programme. The significant hint about the acquiescence of the crown, was at the same time a species of pledge, that the course of innovation would not exceed the patience of a prudent, pious, and orthodox monarch.

The first reform proposed by the new minister, was received by the Liberal party and the Ecclesiastical party in a widely different spirit. The Liberals called it : " Saving the Common School System of Prussia." The Churchmen, both Catholic and Protestant, said it was " The surrender of the schools to Materialism and Infidelity." In both phases, as in partisan statements is generally the case, there is a palpable exaggeration, as well as an element of truth. The schools of Prussia were half a century old. They had proved themselves, on the whole, the most efficient in Europe ; and their fruits, by which they are chiefly to be known, were part of every achievement in letters or science, part of every victory in war. Their scope was unquestionably narrow, and their spirit timid in the extreme. They were more distinguished, perhaps, for the method and the discipline which produced an educated people, than for the freedom and breadth of treatment which develop original genius. But the correction of faults cannot always be called the salvation of the subject. The modifications made by Dr. Falk's bill, which aimed, by reducing the controlling influence of the clerical element, to give the schools a more secular character, and to strike at one great source of strength in the Catholic Church, were just and expedient, and they have our cordial sympathy; but it is not easy to recognize a revolution in their modest provisions. The complaints of the Ultramontanes, on the other hand, were both extravagant and absurd. To cut the lower schools loose from the leading strings of a jealous and bigoted ecclesiasticism, and to put them in the hands of men selected only on a scientific basis, would not have been a surrender to infidelity and Atheism. But the government did not go even so far as this. It simply resumed that active supervision, which the constitution claimed for the State, but which had ceased to be more than an empty form. The State did not affirm that thenceforth the teachers should be required to abjure the Mosaic account of creation, nor did it aim at excluding religious instruction at all from the curriculum. Public opinion is not ripe for that in Prussia. The aim of the bill, in short, was to shut out of the schools teachers who were not, first and absolutely, servants of the State and loyal. As laws must be general, this one, of course, curtailed the authority of the Protestant as well as of the Catholic clergy.

The defence of this bill was, also, the occasion of Dr. Falk's *début* as a parliamentary leader. It was by no means his first parliamentary experience. He had sat in the Prussian House of Deputies from 1858 to 1861, in the Constituent North German *Reichstag* in 1867, and he had been a member of the Imperial Parliament from the first. At one time he was Clerk or Secretary of the House. In these days, however, he was mainly a silent member, and won only the modest renown of punctual attendance. It was, therefore, with some curiosity that the politicians awaited the first appearance of the new minister. Although the Liberals, his friends, were largely in the majority in the Lower Chamber, the opposition numbered many practised debators, who, as the servants of an infallible spiritual master, were apparently placed above those restraints of moderation, courtesy, and truthfulness, which apply in secular relations. Mallinckrodt and Windthorst and Reichensperger were amply endowed with means and inspired with zeal for the defence of a hopeless cause. They made a prodigal use of invective, in the name of a Church which teaches the virtue of humility and forbearance. They led their hearers into tortuous mazes of sophistry; they wrapped the subject in clouds of paltry fallacies, at the command of bishops whose gospel is light. They seemed, in fact, to imitate the manners of Santa Clara, and the dialectics of Schiller's Domingo.

The subject of these debates, too, was of the most comprehensive, intricate, and recondite description. It included Church history from the Fathers to the council of the Vatican; dogmas, decrees, and encyclical letters; the theology of politics and the politics of theology. Examples ranged between the extremes of an Emperor who knelt at the feet of a triumphant Pope, and of a Pope who was imprisoned at the command of a military dictator. Invective was turned now upon the tyranny and violence of princes whom the Church would have purified, and now upon the annals of a spiritual throne, which has been disgraced by the vilest men and the gravest crimes. It was no uncommon thing to see an afternoon spent on an obscure feature of a Council of Trent or of Nice. The Ultramontanes in particular were fond of theological and canonical disputes, on which they were, of course, better informed, and in which they could parade *ad populum* panoramic stores of learning. For any sudden manœuvre of the foe over this vast field of action, the Liberals were bound to be prepared.

To meet the necessities of such a campaign against such valiant soldiers, the government had indeed a variety of leaders. The chief of the National Liberals, Lasker, a fluent and popular orator, spoke for the great middle class represented by the Left, in the language of a philosophical patriot. Dr. Gneist treated the legal issues in the style and with the authority of a professional jurist. The helmet of Bismarck, like the white plume of Harry of Navarre, was always seen where the fray was thickest. But the brunt of the struggle—the original vindication, the patient defence, the conciliation of friends, and the reply to particular foes—in short, the conduct of details as the responsible minister, fell to the part of Dr. Falk.

The '*Cultus-Minister*' is a man of about medium height and proportions, with a full black beard, and the heavy eyebrows which often indicate energy and determination. In fact, he has given satisfactory proofs of both these qualities. As regards his energy, an idea of what degree was necessary may be gathered from the foregoing account of his duties, while his courage has stood the ordeal required of every statesman who excites the hatred and exposes himself to the vengeance of the pupils of the Jesuit Mariana. He has been threatened with assassination quite as often as the Emperor and Bismarck. In one pigeon-hole of his desk, a visitor would doubtless find a bundle of threatening communications, carefully registered, filed, and tied up with red tape; and they testify to his official fidelity not less clearly than the flattery of formal praise. Dr. Falk's style of speaking, too, is that of a man not easily frightened. His manner is more aggressive and pronounced than that of Prince Bismarck, although his printed speeches are not so full of rugged epigrams and pointed retorts. Of the two men he is the better debater, but not the better leader. His style a German would call too "objective." He defends his cause too much like an advocate, as if in the performance of a prescribed duty, or even for the glory of a forensic triumph. It is not his nature to reveal the personal feelings and experience that connect him with the cause, nor to appeal to the broad patriotic interests which awaken and sustain enthusiasm. He is always associated with the details, Bismarck with the spirit of the conflict. He is the minister in charge of a portfolio to which the clerical question happens to belong, while Prince Bismarck is the statesman and the responsible champion of the political issues at stake.

It will be easily understood that the Minister of Public Worship, in such a State as Prussia, should be often questioned about the particular form of worship which he himself affects or favors. There was not much doubt about Dr. Von Mühler. He never rose above the literal language of the Augsburg Confession, and he interpreted that instrument in such a spirit of sacerdotal reverence, that even the Catholics were satisfied. They were not solicitous about his succession. For them Dr. Falk was a person anathematized from the start; and they were amused but not interested, when the zealous Protestants tried to extort from him a confession of faith. A satisfactory confession was, I think, never obtained. Dr. Falk administers his office as a jurist and not as a theologian; and demands that his measures be criticised on their merits, without reference to their author. If, however, a creed be required, it would perhaps be found not far from that of the great Schleiermacher. It has been observed that the elder Falk was a liberal theologian, and a dutiful son would certainly not renounce the paternal faith, when it is shared by so large a portion of his educated countrymen. The example of Schleiermacher proves that a man may make puns, and still be a successful preacher. His system of belief seemed to rest on the axiom that the least degree of belief is the best, that the Christian religion would be just as good without the idea of Christ, and that the noblest end of human effort is the cultivation of *esprit*. Dr. Falk and Dr. Hermann and other jurists holding semi-ecclesiastical positions may not accept all the lengths of such a system. They, doubtless, profess a vague acquiescence in the general doctrines of the New Testament; but, in a thorough test, they would be found nearly as far removed from the orthodoxy of Lutheranism as from that of Rome, and this is a fact to which the old school Protestants will never become reconciled. Since Dr. Falk became Minister, in January, 1872, nearly a score of acts have helped to swell the literature of the ecclesiastical contest. Two or three of these were imperial measures, for which, indeed, a Prussian minister is not responsible. The others, which stretch over a course of about three years, were drawn up under the direct supervision of Dr. Falk, were severally submitted by him to the Prussian *Landtag*, and by him were piloted successfully through both houses. The mere enumeration of these measures is like the history of a century.

In the first place, as above stated, he rescued the common schools from the control of the religious sects. Two months later, in May, four great and almost revolutionary measures were presented. One laid down an obligatory course of training under the supervision of the State for all candidates for holy orders; another forbade the exercise of other than purely spiritual discipline by Church authorities; a third instituted a special court for the trial of clerical offenders; a fourth made easier the path of a seceder from one Church to another.

In 1874, the battle began with an act regulating the administration of vacant Catholic dioceses. The way had been previously made clear for these measures by an act abolishing Articles Fifteen and Eighteen of the Prussian Constitution,—guaranty articles for the benefit of the Church. The act introducing obligatory civil marriage was a blow at an ancient prerogative of the Church, which had been abolished nearly everywhere else. The latest, and in some respects the most sweeping, bills were that for the suspension of all State endowments and contributions for the Roman Catholic Church and that for the expulsion of all Catholic religious orders. I have not mentioned a number of minor acts, which were amendatory or explanatory of previous legislation.

In the months of June and July, 1875, Dr. Falk made a long journey through the region of the Lower Rhine. That is the seat and center of the most intense, active, and aggressive Ultramontane spirit, the district which sends the ablest Catholic deputies to Berlin, which nourishes the most influential priests and prelates. It is a region in which one might stone the prophets of the secular power. It could hardly be expected, at least, that a Cabinet minister making a prosaic tour of inspection through a hostile country, should be prepared for a series of popular ovations, such as might be accorded to a king or a victorious general; and the demonstrations in his honor are therefore the more significant, as they seem to have been purely spontaneous.

The series of festivities began at the old Episcopal City of Trèves, and followed the minister down the Rhine. At Bonn there was a banquet, at which Professor Bona-Meyer presided, and at which Dr. Falk made a long speech of thanks. The *Bonner Zeitung* said: "Truly this man has won the hearts of this whole province, through his amiable and striking individuality." The next evening the students of the university organized a monster torch-light procession, which, after parading through the city with songs, halted in front of Dr. Falk's hotel. There was a speech of welcome from a student, to which the guest replied. It may be known that the University of Bonn has also a faculty of Catholic theology, to which the Minister of Education, much to the indignation of the Ultramontanes, had appointed two Old Catholic professors. The students of this faculty naturally held aloof from any honors that were paid to that great foe. In allusion to this Dr. Falk said during his speech: "I know that this illumination is in honor of that *Cultus-Minister* on whom the present time has imposed such arduous tasks, and I do not wonder that a portion of your number hold back. And in fact, if this had not been the case, I should have had doubts. The satisfaction would perhaps have been greater. But, gentlemen, I hold it to be undesirable that, at this time, the conviction should gain ground in the circles which are not represented here, that I deserve the honor of a torch-light demonstration. I do not know whether those circles will ever come to recognize, in my time, that what has been done by me in the name of his majesty the Emperor, was their cause also. But of this I am thoroughly persuaded ; that many bitter, insulting words, which I have been forced to hear during these days, will some time change themselves into a chorus of accord and gratitude."

Similar ovations were accorded to the minister at Cologne, at Düsseldorf, at Aix-la-Chapelle, at Essen, at Duisburg, and other cities in the Rhine provinces. He made two or three speeches in each place, always short but always fresh, pregnant, and pointed. If he is not the man to enchant an audience by poetical thoughts in melodious periods, he gratifies all serious men by a sturdy spirit of zeal and patriotism. The journey undoubtedly led to a wide increase in his popularity.

III.

DR. DELBRÜCK.

THE name of this gentleman doubtless appears in print as often as that of any other German politician, after Bismarck himself. He who reads the stereotyped reports of the sittings of the *Bundesrath*, or Federal Council, will learn that the President of the Imperial Chancelry presided; he who watches the reports or proceedings of the Imperial Parliament, will meet Dr. Delbrück as the representative spokesman of the *Bundesrath*. The former body corresponds to a Senate in some respects, to a Privy Council in others. Made up of delegates appointed and instructed by the several States, it is at once a ministry to whom the preparation of bills belongs, and, at the same time, a regular factor in imperial legislation. As one of the delegates of Prussia, Dr. Delbrück has a regular seat, and, as the *alter-ego* of the Chancellor, he occupies the chair of President.

When a bill has been accepted by the *Bundesrath*, and laid before the Parliament, the former body becomes a sort of responsible ministry charged with the conduct of the measure. It must be explained and defended; objections must be met and amendments considered; and, when necessary, the spirit of compromise must have an authorized representative. If the bill be on a technical subject, military or financial, for instance, some special talent is sent up to the House by the council. On military matters it would be the War Minister Kamecke; on financial matters, it would be Camphausen; on judicial affairs, it would be Leonhardt or Faustle. In any case, however, even if Bismarck himself be present, the President of the Chancelry sits out the debate from beginning to end. No accumulation of papers at his table prevents him from following the proceedings on the floor, and from taking up the subject at any point where his intervention may be prudent or necessary. In the absence of Prince Bismarck, his is the last and the weightiest word. After that comes the call of the House. Nor is this all that parliamentary institutions ask of this industrious man. It also falls to him to respond to all the interrogatories that the curiosity or malice of deputies may suggest, and this requires a sort of information almost encyclopedic. The inquiries range of course over the whole domain of imperial affairs. That one man should be able to master so many subjects, is itself a mystery, but that the same man should also find time to spend several hours a day listening to debates and waiting to answer questions, suggests almost a prodigy.

The personal and official record of Martin Friedrich Rudolph Delbrück is not brilliant or striking. His father was the private tutor of the late King Frederic William IV. and of his present majesty—a worthy and devoted old court servant. Martin was born in 1817, at Berlin, just when the city, as the royal residence, was recovering from the effects of the French occupation and the neglect of its own sovereign. After the usual preliminary courses at the common schools and the gymnasium, he took up the subject of law; and studied not only at the University of Berlin, which had been opened in 1811, through the efforts of Wilhelm von Humboldt, but also at the sister schools of Halle and Göttingen, both then very renowned. It does not appear, however, that he ever became a practical jurist. In 1842, he entered the public service as an assistant in the ministry of Finance, and in 1848, became chief of a bureau of division in the Ministry of Commerce. In this capacity he gave special attention to the commercial relations between the separate States of Germany, and to the subject of the Zollverein. He was more successful in promoting commercial unity, than some of his ambitious colleagues were in promoting political unity. The Frankfort Diet produced at best a nondescript system with its *Reichsverweser* and poor Archduke John of Austria as the incumbent, but in the domain of commerce and customs real and durable work was accomplished. In 1851, the States of Hanover, Oldenburg, and Schaumburg-Lippe joined the Zollverein by a treaty negotiated by Delbrück. In the next decade he negotiated treaties of commerce with France, Belgium, Austria, and Italy, and took an active part in the extension of the Zollverein. Since 1866, the frequent political changes in Germany have required as frequent changes in commercial and fiscal relations, and in all such Delbrück has played a leading rôle. His experience of the practice and principles of commercial administration; his patience, industry, and clearness, and his surprising mastery of details, render him one of the most efficient of men in that honorable and difficult service. There is not much chance for political *coups de théâtre* or sensational displays of any sort in this work. The man of facts and figures is the modest hero, and Delbrück is a man of facts and figures.

It is not surprising that Delbrück was invited to aid in the reconstruction of the Empire. One of the most important conditions of a durable union was a good adjustment of the new fiscal and commercial relations that would result from such an union; questions of revenue, taxation, customs, appropriations, balances were to be examined and answered, and a special sort of talent was required. The jealousy of Bavaria was to be conciliated, and the selfishness of other States, defeated. Immediately after the first impulse that led to the new union at Versailles had given way to an interval of reflection, obstacles and difficulties began to arise, which could only be met by prudence and forbearance. It is generally agreed that Delbrück deserved great praise for his part in this delicate affair. Prussia may have had more brilliant and showy envoys, but she had none who combined in a higher degree the original qualities of the safe negotiator, and the acquired breadth of special and general information.

Dr. Delbrück, like Dr. Falk, has no reputation as a parliamentarian aside from his ministerial functions. He holds, and has held, since 1873, a seat in the Prussian House of Deputies, but official prudence or modesty has hitherto kept him silent. It is no reflection on his modesty to give the greater weight to motives of official prudence. As Dr. Falk never speaks in the Imperial Parliament, even when ecclesiastical questions are before the House, so Delbrück, whose relations are wholly imperial, is careful before Prussian Deputies not to compromise a superior who is at once Chancellor of the Empire and Minister-President of Prussia. It is a fault of the German system that the Legislators for Prussia are thus deprived of his counsels. There is a large class of questions, fiscal and economical, which in their details are national rather than imperial, and on which, in their Legislative treatment, the experience and knowledge of Delbrück would throw much valuable light; but he is practically confined to the honorable but modest support of his vote.

It will give a clearer impression of Herr Delbrück, as well as of the system of which he is a part, if we sketch a typical scene in the Imperial German Parliament. The building dedicated to the use of that august assembly is a triumph of the economy, or the poverty, of the nation. It is far more imposing than the Foreign Office, far less so than the War Office, which is its neighbor in the Leipzigerstrasse. The front part and the upper story are occupied by the library, the reading-rooms, and the clerks offices; the hall claims the chief part of the central building. This hall is noted alike for the absence of ventilation and the want of acoustic effect. As one looks down from the gallery, the first object that strikes the eyes is probably a flag that was presented to the first *Reichstag* by German citizens of New Orleans. The second would be the nervous but popular President, Forckenbeck, flanked by the secretaries. The third, in the absence always of Prince

Bismarck, would be the President of the Chancery, the subject of this sketch, Dr. Delbrück.

In the parliamentary practice of Europe, the interpellation, or question addressed from the floor to the ministers, plays a very important part. It is often, of course, a serious expedient for learning facts; it is often used on a hint from ministers themselves to give them occasion for a desired statement or explanation, but it is, perhaps, oftenest the instrument of which the opposition can annoy and perplex the government. And there are as various forms of response as of the question itself. In another volume of this series, Mr. Gladstone's manner has been compared with Lord Palmerston's. That of Prince Bismarck depends on the subject, the questioner, the hour of the day, and the condition of his own temper. In general, he satisfies curiosity, if at all, in a courteous and practical manner. If, however, as is most often the case in non-political matters, he turns the business over to Delbrück, the spectators are treated to an useful lesson in the parliamentary arts.

Dr. Delbrück is a man about as large and about as stout as the late Governor Andrew of Massachusetts. As he dresses he appears a little more slender. Instead of affecting the classical mantle, which did not improve Governor Andrew's figure, either in life or in Mr. Gould's statue, Herr Delbrück trims his elastic little body in the neatest of coats and the closest of trousers. He is very bald, and as one looks down upon him from the gallery, the top of his head shines like a silver plate, or like the gold snuff-box which he himself taps and opens at frequent intervals. He is deliberate and exact in all his movements. The most unexpected question never finds him unprepared; the most persistent and impertinent curiosity never ruffles the serenity of his manner. The writer has seen him respond to a long series of questions on the most diverse subjects, without apparently the least note of warning or consequently the least special preparation. He always gives information. He can state off hand the probable receipts from the malt tax, the chapter which the *Bundesrath* has reached in the codification of the civil code, the course of negotiations for a treaty of commerce with Monaco, the number of miles in the Bavarian railway system, the height of the mountains in the Saxon Switzerland, the probable governmental policy toward the Rhine in the next century,—so broad is the scope of his acquirements. I sometimes think that he could state what form the French Government will have at the end of the next twelve-month.

He is, however, no prophet. It has been doubted even whether he possesses ideas, and it certainly seems to be no part of his duties to have them. He is pre-eminently a man of facts. His mind is so burdened with exact knowledge, that ideas, even if there were time to generate them, could hardly find a resting-place. In answering a question in Parliament he might be taken for a professor of mathematics reciting a familiar problem in geometry. Rising slowly, and without a trace of the confusion which the questioner, perhaps, hoped to create, he clears his throat, assumes an easy posture, and then in a dry, formal tone begins his reply. "Meine Herren!" This is the genuine bureaucrat. There is no embarrassment, no enthusiasm, no emotion of any sort. The house listens respectfully, but with as little feeling as if it were reading the statement in a journal, instead of hearing it from the lips of a responsible minister.

On only one occasion, within my recollection, has the *Reichstag* tried to shake Delbrück's position. It was last winter, during the debate on the Banking Bill. In the progress of unification the time, of course, arrived for an imperial system of banking and finance ; and pursuant to a resolution of the *Reichstag*, the Federal Council, or a committee of the same, presented the draft of a Bank Act. Now, for all bills thus offered by the Government there is a sort of divided responsibility. The Special Councilor, or member of the Federal Council appointed to the charge of the subject, is always re-enforced by Delbrück as the general representative of the Imperial Chancelry. In the case of the Bank Bill, Camphausen, as Prussian Finance Minister, and Delbrück played the two parts. It soon appeared, however, in the course of the debate that, while those two politicians were thoroughly in harmony about the bill, the responsibility for its objectionable features could be fastened upon neither. The defect in the measure was the failure to provide for a national central bank. On this the Liberals and a portion of the Conservatives insisted with great vehemence, and they assailed the twin champions of the bill with all the parliamentary weapons at their disposal. Delbrück was less obnoxious than Camphausen. Even his enemies respect his zeal, and industry, and efficiency ; and on this occasion, they rebuked not his own theories so much as his alleged subserviency to Camphausen. Still he was pretty roughly handled, and, in spite of his imperturbability, doubtless felt the shock. A way was ultimately found for introducing the desired amendment without a direct legislative affront for the two gentlemen, and concord was restored. During the general debate Delbrück made two long speeches which were able and exhaustive.

The oratorical exploits of such a man offer few moments of dramatic interest. His functions and his nature alike forbid him those flights of fancy, those appeals to the emotions and the passions, which alone would excuse the translation and reproduction here of any of his speeches. Dr. Delbrück is interesting as a part of a system or a machine, of which the world knows perhaps too little. He is, in other words, the typical bureaucrat of Prussia. In the notice of Dr. Falk, I have explained how that gentleman became an independent minister because he was too original to remain chained to a subordinate desk. Delbrück is too much of a martinet wholly to renounce the slavery of red-tape and sealing wax. Falk is a man of genius, who has become a successful minister. Delbrück is a man of talent, who has only become the first of clerks.

The friendship of Delbrück and Camphausen, like that of Damon and Pythias, is too close and touching to escape the chronicler of the times. Political, personal, and social sympathy binds them together. The local wits, until a late period, were fond of drawing the two veterans, seeking relief, after the labors and vexations of the day, in a common and comfortable dinner at the Berliner Club. They were both wifeless, and sought in each others' society a substitute for domestic joys. This pleasing state of things was rudely interrupted in the Spring of 1875. At that time, Dr. Delbrück became the husband of an excellent lady, and the Minister of Finance has never since seemed happy.

Delbrück is known as a pronounced free-trader. In the treaties that were negotiated under his direction the most liberal principles of trade found assertion. He is neither a Cobden nor a Chevalier; and he by no means enjoys, as the former came before his death to enjoy, the honor of conquering a whole nation to his opinions. Although the doctrines of free trade have for many years been fairly respected in German policy, they have by no means such an unquestioned supremacy as in England. There are two great parties, that of free-trade being in a large majority. Delbrück is simply a member of a party, of which, by virtue of official position and advantages, he has become one of the leaders. Of course, this gives the protectionists a grievance against him. In the protectionist press, and in protectionist circles, it is common to speak of the "Duumvirate" Delbrück-Camphausen, as the source of all industrial or monetary evils that afflict the State, and, therefore, as public enemies to be pursued with fire and sword. In the case of Camphausen, who is stout and sluggish, the application of fire at least would make him very uncomfortable. But it may be doubted whether it would have much effect on Delbrück. He would emerge from the flames a little singed, perhaps, and with ruptures here and there in his tegumentary garments; but he would resume at once the course of parliamentary business, and his first words would be, "Meine Herren."

IV.

HERR CAMPHAUSEN.

———•••———

HERR CAMPHAUSEN is a politician who nearly became a banker, and looks like an English peer with plenty of money and the gout. If in his own character he disproves the theory, which came to light in the Tichborne case, that stout men are always dull, he likewise shakes the popular belief in their amiability. In him, good living and corpulency have produced the unusual result of a dyspeptic cynic. It would be incorrect to call him a grumbler. To grumble is an act of impatience as well as of ill-temper ; it is the protest of a person against a state of things which he is unwilling to endure but is powerless to correct. The Prussian Minister of Finance is not a helpless or a weak man. He is not even critical, captious, or meddling. But he resents interference with his own work, and even fair criticism of his own plans, as jealously and as ruthlessly as Mr. Lowe. Here, however, the parallel ends. Mr. Lowe, as a scholar and a wit, entertained the house even in his most blood-thirsty moods; Herr Camphausen is simply brutal without any milder quality to make the brutality palatable. True, he is ranked as a practical financier, and is not ignorant of the principles of his chosen department. But there are other financiers in Prussia. Now and then some of them are elected to Parliament, and ought they to be scolded and cudgeled because they criticise Herr Camphausen's budgets?

The prudence with which the brothers Camphausen conducted their own affairs first called attention, I believe, to their probable capacity for the affairs of the State. The older brother was president of the *Handelsgericht*, or Tribunal of Commerce, at Cologne; and, what is quite unusual in Prussia, he never climbed the hierarchical ladder on his way to the cabinet. He first won distinction as an opposition deputy in the United Assembly. In a moment of weakness, or of sanity, the King, Frederick William IV., invited him into the ministry, of which he became president. It was a cabinet of compromise or conciliation, and has not left a very savory record on the history of the country. His tenure of office enabled him, however, to help his brother Otto along.

Otto was born in 1812, at Hünshoven, near Aix-la-Chapelle. He studied at the gymnasium of Cologne and the universities of Bonn, Heidelberg, Munich, and Berlin. In 1834 he entered the civil service; in 1837 he became an auditor; in 1844 a *Rath;* in 1845 a *Geheimerath*, or privy councilor of finance. His first important legislative work was the preparation of the Income Tax Act, which was laid before the Prussian *Landtag* in 1847. In 1848 he became a diplomat on a small scale. He was attached to the Prussian delegation at Frankfort on-the-Main, which watched over the acts of *Reichsverweser* Archduke John of Austria. As a financier it may be presumed that Camphausen was more concerned with the revenues than the politics of the *Staaten-Bund*. A better school for the political student can hardly be imagined. How to change the *Staaten-Bund* into a *Bundesstaat*, the Confederated States into a Federal State, was the problem of the day, and Camphausen and Bismarck witnessed together the frivolous efforts of the Austrian politicians.

In the year 1858, by one of those hierarchical distinctions which only German usage and language can render, the "Privy Councilor of Finance" became "Superior Privy Councilor of Finance." When an official reaches this point he is but one step from a portfolio on the one hand or a pension on the other. In the case of Camphausen it was a portfolio. He served a few years as President of the "*See-Handlung*," an institution which administered funds furnished by the State for the support and encouragement of commerce. In those days it was in its infancy, and a modest ward of the State. Under judicious management—and not the least judicious was that of Camphausen—it grew rich, powerful, and arrogant; it could almost set the Bank of Prussia at defiance; and within a year or two there have been loud complaints against it as a dangerous institution which has outlived its usefulness.

Baron von der Heydt relinquished the portfolio of Finance in 1869, and Camphausen became his successor. The downfall of the retiring minister had long been imminent. He was a very wealthy merchant, one of those princes of finance or commerce, who are less common in Germany than elsewhere, and who, when they appear, are generally found to have close affinities with their Dutch neighbors over the Rhine. He was one of those equivocal Liberals, so common in the early days of Prussian constitutionalism, who are acceptable to no party. Camphausen was his predestined successor. As chief adviser of Von der Heydt and President of the *See-Handlung*, he was well known to the public as a man who possessed, and he was believed to deserve, the confidence of his Majesty.

He was called a Liberal. The national liberal party, which had been organized after the "reconciliation" of 1866, was in full power in 1869. It classed the new Finance Minister somewhat vaguely as a member. In the parliamentary almanacs he is called an "Old Liberal;" and this designation doubtless pleased him as well as any other. Nobody can say what an "Old Liberal" is. It would seem to describe a politician who prefers to play fast and loose with party ties, appealing with equal fervor to the fraternal sympathies of all factions, and owing a formal allegiance to none. At any rate, an "Old Liberal" must stand in contact with the new or modern liberals; that is to say, with those of the National Liberal Association. As we shall see further on, this state of things has hurt the prestige of the minister in parliament.

From the first moment the new Minister of Finance revealed a very insubordinate and refractory spirit. He is not a foe of constitutional institutions. He accepts them most unreservedly in theory and even in their application to other men, until they begin to disturb his own repose. But to arraign him under their operation, to press parliamentary privileges into the sacred precincts of the Finance Ministry, is an exceedingly hazardous proceeding. This is trespassing on dangerous ground. If the minister in his wrath would only attack the principle of the interpellation, the victim would more easily escape. He would accuse Camphausen of disloyalty to parliamentary law, and thus put him in an attitude of antagonism to the entire House. This is never possible. The replies of the Minister are always full of formal homage to the House, but he lashes the individual offender, who within his rights of course represents the House, with the most cruel and savage retorts. The House laughs while it is most angry. There is about the manner of the minister such a pompous arrogance, such a masterly impudence, that pity is drowned in admiration; and, before the members have sufficiently overcome their amazement to feel their indignation, the subject has been dropped, and the offender is quietly polishing up his gold spectacles. I believe that both the Prussian House of Deputies and the *Reichstag* are afraid of this belligerent person. They now and then criticise him timidly when he is absent, but in his presence their attitude is one of mingled fear and respect which is deeply interesting to the observer.

It has been said of Camphausen, and truly, that he has had the disposition of more money than any Minister of Finance since the Prussian Exchequer was founded. His predecessors were either cramped by the poverty and economy which honorably distinguished the pre-constitutional era, or they were forced, as during the first two decades of the constitutional era, to wrest money from or collect it in spite of hostile parliaments. Camphausen has had little opposition and plenty of money. He came into office as a quasi-liberal in 1869, just when the fruits of the "reconciliation" of the majority with the Government were about to be reaped in further measures of union. Then came the war with France, which silenced the voice of unpatriotic censure. It was an easy thing to satisfy a people who were following events in France instead of studying the measures of the treasury. After the war came the *milliards*.

This, the most prosperous, was at the same time the most critical moment in Herr Camphausen's career. Of the five *milliards* paid by France as indemnity, about two-thirds went to Prussia, and into the hands of the Minister of Finance, while the distribution of the remainder was largely determined by his advice. It is no part of our duty to criticise or even to explain the details of this great financial operation. Nothing like it had ever been known in the annals of civilized States, and this must perhaps be suffered to soften the judgment of the measures to which it gave rise.

It is perhaps not the fault of Camphausen if, in a land where the Prince still reigns by divine right, not a franc of this immense sum was used to lighten the burdens of the people. It was disbursed in the forms of gifts to princes and ministers, for the construction and repair of fortifications, for building military railways and ironclads, and in a measure for hospitals, pensions, and other benevolent interests. It may be urged, of course, that these were necessary works, and that, without the indemnity, an appropriation, and therefore fresh taxes, would have been necessary. This is only partially true. At the end of a costly war the Government would hardly have asked the people to make fresh offerings for the army and the forts. Herr Camphausen was understood to promise a lightening of taxes as a result of the indemnity, but it was never apparent to the country. This diasppointment was a great blow to Camphausen's prestige. Since that operation he has been bitterly hated by the nation at large, and out of favor with the great body of Liberal deputies. This may not have affected in the slightest degree his own satisfaction with himself and with his work. It certainly has not dulled the acerbity of his temper.

The next important measure in which Herr Camphausen was concerned, was the Banking Act of 1874. As this has been mentioned also in the notice of Camphausen's colleague, the President Delbrück, I shall refer to it now only so far as it may seem to bear on the subject of the present sketch. As one of the Prussian delegates to the *Bundesrath*, Camphausen naturally takes a leading part in the preparation of financial measures; and the Banking Bill, as presented to parliament last year, was justly believed to embody, in a large degree, his favorite views. That he was bold enough to discard many of the leading features of Peel's Bank Act, was, at the time, the subject of much comment, as was the chief principle that he himself introduced.

This principle was in general that of taxing surplus circulation. A normal limit to the issue of each bank was fixed; above this point all issues, to another fixed limit, were taxed at the rate of one per cent.; above this second limit a tax of five per cent. was levied. The theory seems to be that in ordinary times the total untaxed circulation will be adequate to the public needs. When, however, there is a demand for more currency it will become *ipso facto* profitable to issue more, even under the one per cent. tax provision. At the same time the ability to pay this tax will be confined to the strongest banks, which are those most desirable in the public interest as banks of issue. In the original bill no provision was made for an Imperial Bank. The Bank of Prussia was to receive its share of circulation like any other bank, but it was as the Bank of Prussia. This the majority corrected in the manner described in another article. The Bank of Prussia was converted into an Imperial Bank, without, however, affecting the right of issue conceded to other banks.

The working of this novel principle in banking is watched with a good deal of curiosity throughout Europe. It is, of course, too early yet to pronounce judgment on its success, for the complete transfer from the old system to an uniform currency is far from being complete, and has not been unattended with difficulties. At the time we write there is great stringency in the money market. The withdrawal of the old Prussian notes has not been followed by the issue of an adequate supply of imperial money, and the circulating medium is not equal to the wants of trade. This is, of course, all referred by popular logic to the Finance Minister himself. On his broad shoulders all the blame is thrown, but on the streets his carriage is as imposing and his mien as sublime as in the most prosperous times.

To complete Herr Camphausen's official record, he was a member of the Prussian *Landtag* from 1849 to 1852, and of the Erfurt Parliament. He was created a member of the *Herrenhaus*, or Chamber of Peers, in 1860, and took his seat in 1861. He became a delegate to the Federal Council in 1870. Two years ago an official pamphlet was prepared with an account of Camphausen's leading achievements as a minister. The Parliamentary Handbook, from which I glean the above facts, observes at the close, that Camphausen's policy has always aimed at lightening the burdens of the poorer classes and adding to those of the wealthier. This would seem to distinguish him from those financiers who maintain that the weight of taxation ought to fall on the poor.

Camphausen is one of the ministers whom, against his will and without his knowledge, the gossips are always sending into retirement. At the time I write, reports of his resignation are again current. These spring, in a measure, from the general dislike in which he is held, and, in a measure, from the belief that the Chancellor does not share all his financial and theoretical views. Prince Bismarck has never pretended to special knowledge of financial subjects. This has of course been a fortunate thing for Camphausen, who has thereby come less seldom into conflict with his chief than the other ministers. In these days, however, a rumor has been in circulation that the Prince was veering round toward protectionist views, and that a policy antagonistic to free trade might, in view of a widespread industrial depression, be introduced in legislative measures. This would necessitate the withdrawal of the Finance Minister. One of the things which even his Liberal critics are not reluctant to praise is his steadfast and intelligent devotion to free trade, and he could not for an instant form part of a government which should demand the sacrifice of that principle.

All this, however, rests on rumor, and Herr Camphausen will probably remain. A man of two hundred and fifty pounds weight, a stubborn will, and an ugly temper, is not easily moved in so conservative a land as Prussia.

PART III.

THE DIPLOMATIC SERVICE.

V.

PRINCE HOHENLOHE.

THE natural and accepted supremacy of Prussia in the German Empire makes it inevitable that her public men should be at the same time the representative public men of all Germany. Deeply as this may be felt by the patriots as well as the separatists of Saxony or Bavaria, it is a political consequence of 1866, confirmed by the events of 1870–71; and it has a moral explanation even more pregnant and obvious than the political. Mere numbers alone would not be adequate. Attica was not the most populous State of Greece, but she furnished the statesmen as well as the poets and philosophers. Prussia has contributed the guiding politicians of Germany, because she educates and trains them. The secret is in that comprehensive bureaucracy, through the degrees of which a candidate for political honors passes as in the army, till he comes forth an experienced political servant. He is likely to be somewhat narrow in his views, and wedded to formulas in his method. But he is at all events trained in the theory and the practice of his profession.

Such a system could not be maintained in a republic. The one permanent, recognized center, around which all revolve, is not found in the person or the office of an elective President. Democracy excites, as it ought to excite, the spirit of initiative—too often, alas, of irresponsible initiative—and this is fatal to an established bureaucratic system, like that of Prussia.

It is a curious fact, and one which confirms the foregoing reasoning, that the one typical non-Prussian statesman, whom we have selected, owes his success in politics in no small degree to the training which he received in the Prussian civil service. Prince Hohenlohe did not begin his career in his native State till he had qualified himself by years of hard work in Prussia. He may, indeed, owe his rapid rise in the councils of the Empire to his escape from the shackles of Prussian routine, but this does not exclude the counter-theory that the discipline of that routine helped him upward in his own State. Herr Brachvogel, one of Hohenlohe's biographers, thinks that the Prince "did not regard the Prussia of that time as the model State, that she was, indeed, far from that degree of political maturity. But the real spiritual, moral, and effective material, out of which alone a good, strong, and influential State is built, was there. This material he had, as an official, studied in its worst, most crippled, antiquated, and helpless form, under Eichhorn, and had learned to respect it." * It is this man, now German Ambassador at Paris, and one of the most trusty advisers of Prince Bismarck, who is the subject of the following pages.

---

* Brachvogel: Die Männer der Neuen Deutschen Zeit. Vol. III.

The family Hohenlohe traces itself back as far as Gisbert, Duke of East Franconia, who was converted to Christianity about the middle of the seventh century. It is customary, however, to regard as the head of the family Hermann the Illustrious. His son changed the name Rothenburg to Hohenlohe. His son again, Siegfried—and this is a curious fact in view of recent events in the life of our Hohenlohe—this Siegfried was one of the suite of the Emperor Henry IV., when that monarch went to Canossa to humble himself at the feet of the Pope,* but returned to Germany before the performance of the humiliating act. The line continues down to the year 1553, when it was divided into a Protestant and a Catholic branch. The present statesman belongs to the latter. We have traced his descent thus in some detail, not for any interest that such genealogical questions for their own sake may have for our readers, but because of two remarks that in Hohenlohe's case they always suggest. The first is, that a noble of his exalted family connections should voluntarily enter and pursue, like any plebeian, a long course of training in the civil service of Prussia. The other remark was made at the time of Hohenlohe's appointment to Paris, and to the effect that the selection of one of the most powerful and illustrious nobles of Germany was a compliment to France, out of which the best auguries might be extracted.

Chlodwig Carl Victor was born on the 31st of March, 1819, on the family estate of Schillingsfürst, in Bavaria. He had four brothers, one older, the present Duke of

---

* Brachvogel.

Ratibor, and three younger, one of them being Cardinal Hohenlohe, and another a Chamberlain of the Emperor of Austria. Since the family property had become much reduced, and Chlodwig as second son could not claim the title and honors of the house, he resolved to seek his own fortune in the most democratic way. After studying politics and law at the universities of Göttingen, Heidelberg, and Bonn, he began at the bottom-round to climb the official ladder of the Prussian service. *"Auscultator," "Referendar," "Assessor,"* these titles represent to a Prussian the steps in his progress. In 1840, or thereabouts, his brother became heir to a large estate by a collateral line, and was made Duke of Ratibor. Chlodwig might have become head of the Schillingfürst line and a *Fürst* (Prince). To the astonishment of his friends and the vexation of the Bavarians he preferred to stick to his briefs and deeds, and the next younger son, Philip Ernst received the dignity. Five years later, however, Chlodwig seems to have thought his hour was come. Philip Ernst died, and the elder brother finally took possession of the family estates, and became Fürst von Hohenlohe-Schillingfürst. He retired from the Prussian service, and assumed the dignities and duties of his new position in his native land. The period of training ends here, and that of action begins.

As head of a noble family, Fürst Hohenlohe enjoyed the honors of a *Reichsrath*, and a seat in the Upper Chamber of the *Landtag*. Parliamentary life was not then active in Bavaria. The State was in a transition state from feudalism to constitutionalism; and in fact Hohenlohe himself was the reporter of a bill which aimed at making this transition more rapid and sure. In 1848 the imperial or "*Bundes*" government at Frankfort-on-the-Main invited him into the diplomatic service. He filled the position of ambassador successively at Athens, Florence, and Rome. In 1849 he was offered a portfolio in the Bavarian ministry and declined it. Having passed his "Lehrjahre," * he was now anxious to complete his "Wanderjahre;" and too early an entry upon cabinet work would not have been reconcilable with his plans. He ended this stage in his career at London. In 1850 he retired from politics and lived with his family on his estate, making, however, from time to time, visits to France, Italy, and England. In 1860 he again took his seat in the *Reichsrath*. Prince William had become King of Prussia, and had already initiated the new policy which was to be so vigorously and successfully pursued by Bismarck. During these years, and up to 1866, but one issue divided parties in Bavaria, the rival claims of Austria and Prussia to the Bavarian alliance. The extreme Catholic or Ultramontane faction, the so-called patriots, and, it must be said, the majority of the nation, inclined to the former. A smaller party, mostly Protestants and Liberals, represented the Prussian interest. Hohenlohe was the leader of this party. In his speeches and all his public acts he persistently maintained that the hope of German unity lay in Prussia, and up to Sadowa itself, he warned his countrymen against the fatal consequences of a league with Austria.

---

* The German mechanics pass through a period of apprenticeship, called the "Lehrjahre," and a period of traveling called the "Wanderjahre." Goethe's "Wilhelm Meister" is founded on this practice

When, after the close of the war, the Minister Von der Pfardten came before the Chamber to ask the ratification of the treaty of peace, Hohenlohe declared, under the applause of the House, that "the ratification of the treaty of peace must be the last political act of the ministry, and only by the immediate retirement of this cabinet can the country recover from its severe trial." After this no successor but Hohenlohe was possible. On January 1st, 1867, he became Premier of Bavaria and Minister of Foreign Affairs. His policy in German politics he explained in the Chamber by the following remark: "I hold it to be more expedient now, while everything is in motion, while things are adjusting themselves, to take a position towards the North German Confederation whereby it is possible to secure favorable conditions for the independence of Bavaria and her dynasty—I hold this to be more expedient than to knock at a finished house, of which the doors are already locked." He also drew up for the information of the King a long memorandum of the policy which would govern him as minister.

In August, 1867, he carried through the *Landtag*, by clever parliamentary strategy, a treaty of alliance, offensive and defensive, with Prussia, as well as a commercial treaty amounting to a Zollverein. When the Zoll or Customs Parliament met at Berlin in 1868 it recognized Hohenlohe's services by electing him president.

The most important service rendered by Hohenlohe was, nevertheless, against the Church of which he was a member, to which the great majority of the Bavarian people belonged, and in the Holy College of which his brother sat as a cardinal. To him belongs the honor of first grasping the significance of the Council of the Vatican. While even Prince Bismarck was inactive, and his Minister at the Vatican, Harry Von Arnim, was coquetting with Jesuits and priests, and long before any other power had taken any active measures against the pending revolution, Prince Hohenlohe, the minister of little Catholic Bavaria, had mastered the situation and was trying to teach it to Europe. In March, 1869, he issued a circular note to the representatives of Bavaria abroad. In view of its historical importance, and of the revelation of Hohenlohe's foresight which it affords, I give a complete translation:

Circular Dispatch in Regard to the Council.

"It may now with certainty be assumed that, unless unforeseen obstacles arise, the Œcumenical Council, called by his Holiness Pope Pius IX., will actually meet in December. Without doubt it will be attended by a great number of bishops from all parts of the world, and will be larger than any that has yet taken place; and it will claim for itself and its acts, in the public opinion of the Catholic world, the high respect due to an Œcumenical Council.

"That the Council will occupy itself with purely dogmatic questions, with purely theological subjects, is not to be supposed, since questions of that sort, which demand such a solution, are not at hand. The only dogmatic question which it is hoped may be settled in Rome by the Council, and for which the Jesuits in Italy as in Germany and elsewhere are agitating, is, as I learn from a trustworthy source, that of the infallibility of the Pope. This, however, reaches far beyond the strictly theological domain, and is of the highest political nature, since therewith the fame of the Popes would be elevated over all Princes and people, in secular matters, to an article of faith.

"If, now, this highly important and momentous question is well adapted to direct the attention of all governments, which have Catholic subjects, toward the Council, their interest, or more properly their concern, must be intensified, when they regard the preparation now making and the choice of the committees for this work in Rome. Among these is one to which is assigned exclusively the politico-ecclesiastical matters. It is therefore beyond doubt the intention of the Roman Court that at least some resolutions concerning such matters or questions of a mixed nature, shall be formed by the Council. Hence the *Civiltà Catolica*, the periodical of the Jesuits, which Pope Pius IX. in a special *brève* endowed with the character of an official organ of the Curia, men tioned as a task incumbent on the Council to convert the anathemata pronounced by the Pope on December 8, 1864, into positive resolves or conciliatory decrees. Since these articles of the syllabus are directed at many axioms of political life as developed among all civilized peoples, the earnest question presents itself to the governments, how and in what form they shall convey to their respective bishops, and later to the Council itself, a sense of the serious consequences of such a disturbance of the present relations of Church and State. The question also further arises, whether it be not expedient for the governments in common, perhaps through their representatives in Rome, to enter a caution or protest against such resolves as might be made by the Council independently, without the concurrence of the representatives of the States, without any previous communication over clerico-political questions or those of a mixed nature.

"It appears to me to be imperatively necessary that the States interested try to reach a mutual understanding upon this serious affair. I have hitherto waited to see if a move would not be made from some direction; since this has not taken place, however, I feel it my duty to authorize you to bring the subject up for discussion by the government to which you are accredited, in order to learn its views and feelings.

"You will therefore suggest for the consideration of such government the question, whether common if not united action of the European States, in a form more or less identical, ought not to be taken, in order not to leave the Curia in doubt about their attitude toward the Council; and whether some sort of a conference between the representatives of the interested governments would be the best method of obtaining an exchange of view in regard to that attitude.

"You will leave a copy of this dispatch, if desired, and send report about the spirit in which it is received."

As Hohenlohe foresaw the war with Rome, so he early foresaw that with France. In February, 1870, half a year before the actual declaration of war, he said, in the presence of some political friends: "There can no longer be any doubt that war will break out in the course of this year between France and Germany."* The recent elections had returned a small clerical majority, and though the King offered to retain Hohenlohe, he decided to retire. "If I am at the head of affairs," urged he, "the opposition will refuse, out of hostility toward me, to carry

---

* *Männer der neuen deutschen Zeit.* Vol. III.

out the terms of the alliance with Prussia; but if a particularist [*i. e.*, "states-rights"] ministry be in power, it will be carried away by the popular feeling and do its duty." This statesmanlike theory was carried into effect. On the 13th of February he resigned his office, and Count von Bray, on his advice, became his successor. He did not, however, relinquish all participation in politics. When the war actually broke out he hastened to Munich, and by his counsel kept up the spirits of both King and people.

After the close of the war Hohenlohe took an active part in the organization of the new imperial system. He was chosen to the first Imperial Parliament from his home district in Franconia, and has been regularly re-elected. As a deputy he belonged to the national party, and has steadily supported Bismarck's ecclesiastical and foreign policy. As a faithful, but modest deputy, *Fürst* Hohenlohe served the cause of the Fatherland till 1874, when events, quite as much as the favor of Bismarck, summoned him to a new post of great honor and greater difficulty.

With the circumstances which led to the removal of Count Harry von Arnim from the head of the German embassy at Paris, the public has lately become pretty familiar. Some more details on the subject will be given in the next chapter, on Arnim. But the public was not equally familiar with his successor, and his recommendation for the succession. The secondary rôle necessarily played by the smaller States in imperial politics, and the overshadowing greatness of Bismarck's own name, almost invited the world not to know the obscure but faithful leaders, who, in critical moments, had kept the South German States up to their duty. Prince Hohenlohe was the first of these, but that was only to be first in the second class. The Chancellor, however, knew his man. He knew that if Hohenlohe wanted the versatility of Arnim, he possessed, on the other hand, nearly every qualification that Arnim wanted. He was, in the first place, a man who resolutely put his own fortunes after the welfare of the State, in importance. He had as much foresight as Arnim; but, unlike him, he never mistook his fancy for facts and made it the basis of official action. Years of thorough training had taught him that indispensable spirit of discipline and obedience which is the secret of the Prussian service. His powerful and ancient family connections were not to be overlooked in the candidate for a service which is still highly aristocratic. He being a representative South German, his appointment was a prudent if not a necessary compliment to the loyalty of the smaller States. He was profoundly devoted to the policy of Bismarck. And finally, as the best professional qualification, he had filled diplomatic posts in several important capitals, had traveled much, and knew the manners and men of many countries.

In the summer of 1864, the Prince was appointed to the Paris Embassy, and entered at once on the duties of the position. He was received with pleasure by the French Government, and enjoys in French society as much credit as it is willing to accord to a German. His diplomatic triumphs are yet, indeed, to be won. The peaceful course of affairs between the two nations has given little occasion for any display of ability on the part of the ambassador, but when an emergency arises it cannot be questioned that he will do his duty like a statesman and a patriot.

Prince Hohenlohe was married on the 16th of February, 1847, to Maria, Princess of Sayn-Wittgenstein. Two children are the fruit of this union, Stephan, born in 1851, and Philipp Ernst, in 1853. The Princess takes a keen interest in politics; and by her connections and her encouragement has been a valuable support to her husband's plans.

Herr Brachvogel has a marked and sometimes ludicrous tendency to deify his heroes, but the following account of Hohenlohe's appearance is not very much overdrawn: "There are human countenances, from which an idea of character can be learned only with difficulty, and seldom with certainty. Such a face Prince Hohenlohe has not, for his reveals clearly and truly what the man is and what he is not. The form of the head, the lines of the profile, the position of the lower jaw, make of his portrait what is called a 'fine head.' The superior humanity and repose which speak out of his lineaments, out of his earnest, benevolent, dark glance, give the impression of an ample supply of heart and brain, together with the conviction that they could serve only the purest cause. The muscles of the forehead are very marked, and a result of the mental labor which has been going on beneath in the laboratory of human ideas. The short crisp hair above the high but narrow forehead; the fine lips, which move in harmony with the movements of the eye, and are shaded by a moustache, which hides their involuntary play; and then the delicately slender but not too tall figure, the easy and elegant carriage, characterize the statesman as well as the man of the world.*

---

* Brachvogel, Vol. III., p. 168.

The leading features of his character, as shown by actions, the same writer describes as follows : " We do not believe the Prince could be very violent, nor that he is capable of too transparent humor. His physiognomy is like a thin vail, which never forms too thick folds, which reveals, however, in firm contours, all that passes behind it, in the spirit or the emotions of its owner. To the strong positive knowledge of the Prince is allied the gift of sharp and rapid judgment, clearness of mind, and readiness with the pen ; especially, too, a calm and dispassionate view of facts, a determined grasp on what is held to be right, an incorruptible unselfishness, and yet a tenderness of heart, and the difficult art of conciliating an opponent's opinion."*

This describes pretty nearly a saint in politics, and, of course, some degree of exaggeration must be pardoned to the patriotic enthusiasm of the author. But the tribute to Hohenlohe's benevolence and integrity is not overdrawn. The respect of his enemies, and the admiration of his friends agree in doing homage to a statesman whose private character illustrates the virtues of domestic life as transparently as his official career illustrates those of the citizen and the patriot.

---

* Brachvogel, Vol. III., p. 168.

VI.

COUNT HARRY VON ARNIM.

IF Prince Hohenlohe, the present Ambassador at Paris, is but little known outside of Germany, Count von Arnim is at least notorious. The *cause célèbre* in which he figured as defendant was a scandal that the world will not soon forget; and it was itself enough to assure the Count that questionable sort of fame which the dignity of the nineteenth century does not forbid it from granting to such sensational characters. Thanks to the exactions of a curious public, but few of the details of Count Arnim's life have escaped publication. In the sketch which I shall give of him, however, the reader will not expect, or expecting will not receive, a barren recital of gossip, such as the arrest and trial and sentence of the diplomatist called into being. What is not forbidden by the dignity of history is at least forbidden by respect for a family which has deserved well of its country, and whose least fortunate member was long a trusted servant of his sovereign.

The history of Harry von Arnim is that of a man of aristocratic birth and powerful connection, whose natural advantages had been improved by the best education and the best training that Prussia affords; who entered on his official career with glowing prospects, rising steadily to the most important diplomatic post in his country's service; and who, through too much confidence, leading him from one false step to another, finally arrived in the prisoner's dock of a criminal court, and there stood up before the eyes of the world to be sentenced like a common felon. To-day he is a wanderer in foreign lands and an outcast from the society of his own friends. Sad as is this career, and a sadder one can hardly be found in the records of Germany, it will be for the reader to inquire, after reading the facts, whether posterity is likely to reverse a judgment confirmed by the highest court in Prussia.

The Arnims cannot, like the Hohenlohes, trace their lineage back to the middle ages, but, as a family, I believe they are some two centuries old. The immediate ancestors of Harry were aristocratic but not titled. His grandfather was poor and obscure; but he served his country in one of the most useful of all ways—by raising children. He had no fewer than eleven sons, five of whom fell at the Battle of Waterloo. Harry himself was adopted by his uncle, Heinrich von Arnim. So little was known of the family that Harry was generally supposed to be the son instead of the ward of the so-called "March Minister"—a relationship of which he might indeed have been proud. History moved so swiftly in Prussia during the past decade that new readings are very often necessary. The names of Harry von Arnim and Marshal Manteuffel were once associated as the two leading members of a possible Conservative coalition against Prince Bismarck, but a good many people have probably forgotten that the guardian of the former was a bitter political foe of the latter's brother, and was, like his *protégé*, prosecuted in a police court for a political delinquency. It was in the days of Friedrich Wilhelm IV., and Heinrich von Arnim was one of those who would not go to Olmütz. He was a man of showy talents and a fine speaker. While Manteuffel was away on his humiliating pilgrimage Arnim made a public speech, in which the conduct of Manteuffel was arraigned with all the vigor and eloquence of an indignant patriotism; and the returning minister responded by citing him before the court for the speech. Arnim defended himself by another speech. It was before a couple of judges and half-a-dozen attorneys, and he himself was accustomed to sneer at his audience, but the performance was an admirable one. The ministry forbade its publication, and it was printed in Switzerland. Heinrich von Arnim was in every respect one of the finest characters in modern Prussian history. He was a scholar and an orator, a diplomatist who scorned intrigue, and a minister who was first a patriot. His austere life and grave demeanor won him the sobriquet of the *Bet-bruder* (Prayer-brother). The irreverent thought this was a term of ridicule, but Arnim accepted it as an honor.

With the precepts and example of this excellent man constantly before him, young Arnim passed his youth and early manhood. His studies were made chiefly in Berlin. At the university he was a model man, full of wit and spirits, a leader in literary circles, a good fencer and horseman, and fond of all sorts of manly exercise. He was indeed poor, but he was proud, chivalrous, and popular. Already in those days he was marked for a political career, and when he entered the diplomatic service his promotion was as rapid as could be desired.

He first became known to the world, and therefore an object of popular interest, at Rome. It had been the policy of the Prussian Government to treat the embassy at the Holy See rather as a sinecure, to be confided to elderly *savans* seeking for Latin particles or the origin of Roman civilization, than to active professional politicians. Peace, or at least a truce, prevailed between Berlin and the Vatican. Devout Protestants, with at least a public respect for the Church of Rome, were always acceptable to the Pope. Harry von Arnim was, however, a scholar as well as a politician. His appointment to Rome was in no sense disrespectful to the memory of his learned predecessors, while it unmistakably lifted the mission to the rank of a political post, calling for the service of a trained politician.

The opportunity for political work did not come at first. No disturbing questions were pending for a time, and Arnim enjoyed and improved a city where everything appealed to his taste, his culture, and his scholarship. He made profound studies of ancient Roman art, and mastered, in the spirit of an antiquarian, the history of extinct societies in that wonderful peninsula. He was one of the most popular members of the diplomatic corps. The graces of his person and manner won the admiration of the ladies, his wit and eloquence were prized even by the witty and eloquent Italians, and his real or affected piety revealed to the Vatican the possibility of an illustrious convert. When the assembling of the Œcumenical Council brought the hour for action, the Prussian Ambassador had won a position enjoyed by none of his colleagues.

In regard to the attitude which the State should take toward the Council, it has since been revealed that there was an original difference of view between Arnim and Bismarck. The former explained his theory in the celebrated "Promemoria," addressed to Dr. Döllinger; the latter in the form of instruction to the ambassador himself. In referring to the views of Arnim, so far as is necessary for my purpose, I shall guard against calling him a friend of Ultramontanism. His own published memoranda refute such a charge. But his opposition to Rome was different in intensity, and still more in character, from that of Prince Bismarck and the Liberals of Germany. Count von Arnim abhors Roman Catholic doctrine in the spirit of a Prussian Protestant; Prince Bismarck abhors the Roman Catholic Church in the spirit of a free-thinking, German politician. Arnim would tolerate the Church in the interests of the throne and nobility, if she did not teach too much false doctrine. Bismarck cares nothing about her dogmas and decrees, but a great deal about her power as a social and political factor in Germany. And the lack of harmony between the two at Rome arose just out of this initial difference in political methods. Count von Arnim wished the State to interfere in the Council in order to save the Church from a theological calamity, while Bismarck wished the dogma to be rejected in the interest of the State and society. Arnim saw clearly that the Council, as an ecclesiastical legislature, was wholly in the power of the Italian Jesuits, and he saw, too, what a great many statesmen did not see, that the *non placet* of the German, French, and American bishops would not have the slightest moral effect on the Council, and would not be maintained even by those prelates themselves without the active support of the civil power. His recommendation to the German, or rather the Prussian Government, was, therefore, first, to appoint an agent who should demand the privilege of being present at all sessions of the Council, and second, to make the resistance of the Prussian and German bishops a State cause, to be supported as such. Here was the draft of a distinct policy, which, if adopted, would have wholly changed the relations of the European States to the Council. It is but just to Count von Arnim to say that many men, who are in no special sense his friends, concede to him now a remarkably clear view of the matter at the time, and even believe, in view of the action which the State is now taking toward the Church, that his advice was wise, and ought to have been followed. He was certainly correct in predicting that the German opposition to infallibility would not stand without the aid of the State. Whether the converse be true, as he thought in 1870, and insists to-day, is a problem which will never be solved. Bismarck declined to interfere with the course of legislation at the Vatican, and in two dispatches, which he has since published, he set forth his reasons for leaving things to take their own course, and testifies furthermore to the complete indifference on the subject which then prevailed in Prussia.

That this difference of view did not lead to any personal coolness, seems to follow necessarily from Arnim's transfer in 1871 to Paris, with the title of Count. This was a post of greater difficulty. It was just after the war, when the resentment of the French extended to everything German, and an ambassador needed a rare union of tact and decision, of suavity and firmness. In the judgment of disinterested observers at Paris, who were neither German nor French, Arnim was a zealous and sagacious ambassador. No complaint about his conduct was made till his opinions became irreconcilable with those of Bismarck. When his opinion began to influence his conduct, and to give to the Paris Embassy a tendency quite hostile to the policy of the Chancellor of the Empire, a personal hostility arose, with the results which are now widely known. As soon, however, as the breach came, and the critics began to study and compare the characters of the two men, it appeared that there was an irreconcilable antagonism between them, which made continued harmony very difficult. It was the duty of the present writer a year ago to describe this antagonism, and he sees now very little reason to modify what he then wrote.

Both men belong to the *parvenu* aristocracy. The extreme Conservatives complain very often that Prince Bismarck has never paid them for the suit of clothes they gave him when he took office in the interest of reaction ten years ago. Harry von Arnim was a penniless adventurer till a fortunate marriage gave him wealth and social position. He belongs, like Bismarck, to what may be called the mediatized aristocracy—the aristocracy which has become reconciled to political service under parliamentary institutions, and even to a respectable rate of progress in that line. The similarity does not extend, however, beyond their origin and family circumstances, and in character and manner Count von Arnim is almost the reverse of Bismarck. The Chancellor is a cuirassier, with an extravagant degree of the cuirassier's rude and overbearing affectation. The Ambassador is a civilian, and a polished gentleman. Bismarck is impulsive and despotic; Arnim is composed, courteous, reasonable. The former has the most intellectual force; the latter the more cultivated mind. Arnim would not have fought the Prussian Chambers so stubbornly ten years ago; Bismarck could not bandy Latin syllogisms with Roman cardinals and talk Etruscan art with French *savans*. In his political principles Bismarck has broken entirely away from his class; Arnim was always wavering and irresolute. Bismarck knew the military value of the nobles; but he also knew that there was a great deal of rugged political work for Germany, and that the strong arms of the middle classes were indispensable. Arnim was fastidious and aristocratic, and fond of the ancient splendor of his order; but he was ambitious, and he knew that the gratification of his ambition required at least a formal compliance with the new order of things. His personal tastes were at war with his personal aspirations. He was always grasping for the honors of a constitutional system, yet clinging with one hand to the possibilities of a *Junker* restoration. Between the two men the Emperor doubtless preferred Bismarck. The Chancellor was a rough soldier, who never troubled him with fanciful theories of government, was willing to let him hobnob as much as he pleased with brother princes, and flattered him with the forms while he himself kept the substance of power. Besides, Bismarck was frank and open, and his Majesty is a soldier. But

Arnim was the darling of the real Court party, of the literary spinsters, of the official artists and musicians, of the poets laureate, of the modern nobles who had rushed into the vacuum left by the old aristocracy. He was the Leicester rather than the Sidney or the Raleigh. His wit made him a court favorite, and no one now denies that he enjoyed the strong support of the Empress; but this could not save him from impending ruin.

The exact course of events which led to the final rupture was not known at the time, and has just been revealed in detail by Arnim himself. It appears that the public conjectures were not at fault. No better tribute to the absorbing interest of French politics has lately been afforded, than the fact that a change in the Chief of State at Versailles carried with it the removal and ruin of one of the most peaceful of German diplomatists. For such was indeed the fact. Not only was the government of M. Thiers acceptable to Prince Bismarck, but it was his wish that everything possible within the limits of diplomatic action should be done for the maintenance of that government. Count von Arnim was of an opposite opinion. A devoted royalist, he regarded the overthrow of M. Thiers as a triumph of the monarchical principle, and as a devoted courtier, he felt bound to impress this view upon the Emperor William. He himself has published several communications sent to his Majesty by a more direct route than the Foreign Office. Prince Bismarck was naturally indignant at such a presumptuous attempt to shake his authority, and he resented it with a vigor which recalls his best days. As responsible Minister of Foreign Affairs, he was asked to carry out at Paris a policy which he did not sanction. Of course such a state of things could not continue. The Chancellor wrote that he was worn out by the care of setting himself right with his Majesty against a refractory subordinate, that as Arnim had more leisure, all the advantage was on his side, and that the end must soon be reached. When the occasion came the blow fell. When the Turkish mission was raised to the rank of an Embassy, Arnim was transferred to Constantinople. But he never entered upon the new post. After leaving Paris, and while awaiting instructions for Constantinople, a discovery was made which not only put an end to his Oriental prospects, but led to his arrest, trial, conviction, and disgrace.

This was the discovery that the retiring ambassador had carried away with him from Paris a large number of papers which were believed to belong properly to the archives of the Embassy. Being called on to surrender them, the Count refused. He did indeed return a few, which he said had been taken by mistake; but the rest he claimed as private property, or papers necessary for his defense against further attacks from Bismarck. The correspondence was short and the Count had the last word. But the abstraction of State papers is a penal offense, and the Foreign Office could not stop here.

One day in October, 1874, the city was astounded to learn that a pair of gendarmes had arrested Count von Arnim at Nasserhaide, his country seat, brought him abruptly to Berlin, and locked him up in the common jail. Then his house, desks, and private papers were searched for the missing documents, or for evidence of their whereabouts. After a few weeks of the closest confinement the

Count was transferred to the *Charité* or hospital. Finally he was allowed to remain in his own house under police supervision. The intense interest which the case excited was fed by the press of two hemispheres. In Berlin, men spoke of it with bated breath. All sorts of opinions on the summary manner and on the legality of the arrest were expressed; and while the Liberals and the friends of Prince Bismarck demanded that justice be allowed to take its course, the extreme radicals and the ultra conservatives joined in defense of a man who, as the foe of their common foe, was their common friend. As a matter of fact the regularity of procedure in the case has been vindicated at every point. The apparently arbitrary method was not the less legal under a code in which personal liberty is imperfectly defined, and at the hands of officials whose first notion of law is a literal obedience to the orders of a superior.

With the details of the trial the world is more familiar. It was the writer's privilege and his duty to be a spectator of that judicial exhibition, to breathe for several hours a day the hot and corrupt air of the court room, and to witness the unedifying forensic displays of the counsel. Seldom has a trial of such celebrity been conducted with less dramatic impressiveness. It affords very little mat er for the historian and none for the artist. It was an inquisition of scandal, a parliament of gossip, rich in petty bickering, recrimination, and slander, but fruitless of enduring facts or principles. Arnim conducted himself with defiance but not with dignity. At the end of a week, as is known, the Court, in the person of Judge Reich and two assistants, found the prisoner guilty, and sentenced him to one year's imprisonment. The case was carried on appeal through two stages up to the "*Obertribunal*" or Supreme Court of Prussia; and the substance, though not in each case the form, of the original sentence was confirmed.

In the meantime Arnim had retired to Switzerland, where the final decision has just reached him. What he will do is yet to be seen. But immediately after the judgment of the *Obertribunal* there appeared at Zurich a book, "*Pro Nihilo*," which purported to be a history of the preliminaries to the arrest of Arnim, and contained all the documents that had not already been published. It is, of course, attributed to Arnim himself. The book confirms throughout the current account of the quarrel between him and Bismarck, and even the friends of the former regard the publication as a very grave indiscretion. It was the act of a desperate leader who deliberately burns the only bridge by which he can escape.

Harry von Arnim is now a ruined man, and though he may continue to wield a certain force in German politics, it will only be through the rancor of his friends, in which he will direct, and the influence of patrons still not without strength at Court. But at one time after his arrest it was otherwise. Before the trial, while the arrest was regarded as an audacious political enterprise, which might fail and sweep Bismarck out of office, his persecuted rival was naturally treated as his predestined successor. That Arnim himself believed in such a theory is beyond doubt. He seems to have thought that he might form a great party of congenial spirits and on quite new principles, of which he would naturally be the leader. This party would be as far removed from the peevish bigotry of the *Junkers* as from the hateful Liberalism of Hebrew barristers. It would look to the Old Catholics and the moderate Protestants for its religious tone, to the more pliant and adventurous portion of the nobility for social position, to the great Conservative bankers for the sinews of war, to the uncorrupted literary and professional men for brains and work. It would have been first and foremost a party of gentlemen. And though it would not have disdained for parliamentary purposes the unkempt socialist and the elastic ultramontane, it would have restored the lost dignity of the crown and fortified it by the allegiance of every Conservative place-hunter. That Arnim should have cherished such an ambition is proof of his temerity.

If this were Count von Arnim's only fault, it would, indeed, be easy to excuse him, since temerity is a fault of temperament, of the emotions. A brave man is easily pardoned for rashness; but anybody who reads the published correspondence, and supplements that, as the present writer has done, from other sources of information, must discover in the character of Arnim a degree of frivolity unpardonable in a serious statesman. His whole demeanor was that of the artist. A little scenic effect was justified by Burke, and is not considered unworthy of Bismarck. But there is no country in the world where drawing-room politics, and naturally drawing-room politicians, are held in more contempt than in Germany; and when to the grimaces of a fop are added the flippancy of a punster, a very melancholy combination is the result. Count von Arnim was, indeed, something more than a fop and a punster. But he was nevertheless the victim of his own wit to such an extent that he often failed to draw the line clearly between the clown and the ambassador. Take, for instance, his annotations on the dispatches. Some of his friends vexed their souls over the pretended cruelty of many of Bismarck's dispatches. The sentiment does their hearts more honor than their understandings. There may or may not be wit in Arnim's marginal notes on some of the "cruelest" of those dispatches—that is a question for the critics; but in my opinion, the man who made them was not at the time likely to die of a broken heart. His counsel maintained that the notes proved that at that time Arnim meant to take the dispatches away as his own property. The pretense is not an unreasonable concession to his self-respect. But their existence suggests an ugly doubt whether his grief was so profound as is represented, and whether he did not look on his general difficulty with his superior as a comedy out of which fun was to be extracted. If that be his view of the importance of harmony in the diplomatic service it is difficult to see on what ground he can appeal to his own countrymen or to the world for sympathy. Count von Arnim seems to have had the most unbounded confidence in the power of his own name, or of his connections at Court, to shield him against the punishment of his crime at each and at every stage. There was about this theory a sort of flippancy and arrogance which invited the fate that has overtaken him. It was, at any rate, a reckless theory to set up against the known resolution of Prince Bismarck, and if I have correctly described the prisoner's character, its existence does not imply a consciousness of innocence. At the same time it would be manifestly unjust to hold Prince Bismarck responsible for all the petty indignities which Count von Arnim suffered at the hands of over-zealous officials. It is the curse of Kings, and, under constitutional government, of Ministers, "to be attended by slaves that take their humors for a warrant;" but the Foreign Office was too shrewd, if not too scrupulous, to trespass over the bounds of the law.

Count Arnim is a tall, handsome man, with a heavy black beard and moustache, a mouth which curls with a haughty expression, and eyes that reveal spirit and penetration as well as insincerity. By his first wife he had one son, now a young officer of dragoons, whose filial devotion during the imprisonment and trial of his father won general admiration. The second wife was his cousin, a daughter of Count Arnim-Boytzenberg, Governor of the Province of Silesia. She was owner of a large fortune in her own name, and was able to improve the style of the ambassador's establishment.

PART IV.

THE PARLIAMENTARIANS.

VII.

HERR VON BENNIGSEN.

 PERTINENT and fitting introduction to this article will be an account of a visit which the writer has just made to the German Imperial Parliament. It was a day of the practical and the useful, following a day of dramatic and brilliant interest. On the previous day the House had brought to a close the general budget debate, in which the Chancellor himself, just returned from Varzin, had made a long and important speech, which in its turn provoked replies from the ablest of his foes. Next day began the special debate, which is generally dull and unentertaining. The hall wore a thoroughly ordinary aspect. The members were conscientiously inattentive to the several speakers, and spent their time in reading or writing or chatting. Even the suave and patient President yawned now and then, and looked wearily from the clock which ticked on the opposite wall to the tricolored flag which hung above his head. The ministers and clerks sat listlessly at their desks; and of the reporters, only they

who were obliged to transcribe everything transcribed anything. Nevertheless, this unpicturesque scene was, perhaps, in an artistic sense, a better back-ground to two figures which attracted the writer's attention.

They were standing on the elevated section around the President's desk and, careless of the debate, were conducting an earnest discussion between themselves. One of them was a tall, massive man, with a bald head, and a rough hard face, scarcely lighted by a pair of gray eyes disproportionately small. He was in the uniform of a general of cavalry, and he had the carriage and manner of a soldier. While he was speaking his fingers twitched nervously, but he gesticulated little. Now and then he crossed his hands behind him, stretched his giant frame to its extreme height, and one saw a man whose appearance suggested power quite as clearly as his history reveals it. His companion was a man nearly as tall and quite as stout, but the resemblance ends here. For in place of the showy military uniform, he wore clothes which were plain even for a civilian; his complexion was dark, with the tint of the Semitic rather than the Latin race; and he looked out of a pair of heavy, black, piercing eyes. Of all American statesmen he most suggested Mr. Morton. A strong, effective man, deliberate, but not awkward in his movements, earnest and emphatic in his manner. The two seemed not only to be personal friends, but also to have many points of political confidence and sympathy; and the fancy of the spectator could easily rise to the theory that their conversation was ranging through the very gravest questions of state. The first of these two men was Prince Otto von Bismarck, Chancellor of the German Empire, the other was Rudolph von Bennigsen, Speaker of the Prussian Lower House, and member of the Imperial Parliament.

A writer in the *Gartenlaube*, a weekly illustrated periodical, says : " If one is present at the many interesting debates of the present session of the Prussian House of Deputies, one sees in the president's chair, which Herr von Forckenbeck has hitherto filled with so great honor, a man whose aristocratic, stately figure and intelligent lineaments involuntarily attract attention. The whole appearance bears the type of the North German nature, and impresses less through striking qualities, through glowing individuality, through convincing eloquence, through brilliant wit, than through practical readiness, a harmonious development, and manly strength, which demand and deserve confidence and respect. The firmness and calmness with which the new president guides the often too stormy deliberations, the impartiality which on such occasions he shows, the dignity which he always preserves for himself and the House, suggest a long parliamentary career, a firm character, and a marked political talent." *

Von Bennigsen stands in German history as the type of an efficient patriot. His case shows what may be accomplished for political ends by extra-political methods. Although he has spent years in the public service, and sitting in three different legislatures has wielded much influence since 1855, his great work was accomplished by popular agitation outside of the sphere of official action. The *Deutsche National Verein*, or German National Union, of

---

* *Die Gartenlaube*, 1874. p. 93.

which Bennigsen was the founder, held toward the struggle for German unity the same relation as the Concord minute men to the American Revolution—it was the zealous and patriotic levy of hasty forces, which, with the introduction of order and method, gracefully accepted the duty of discipline and subordination to authorized leaders. It was an unofficial but not illegal association. While a timid King of Prussia refused to place himself at the head of the popular cause, and become the center of that unity for which the Fatherland was striving, the *National Verein*, a voluntary association of patriotic and liberal men, organized public spirit and kept alive the hopes of the country. So long as there was no governmental control of the popular efforts, this *Verein* acted as leader; when the State assumed the lead the *Verein* retired.

Rudolph von Bennigsen was born on the 10th of July, 1824, at Lüneburg. He belongs to an old noble Saxon family, which had afterward settled in Hanover, where it seems to have held a good position. He studied jurisprudence at Göttingen and Heidelberg, qualified as an advocate but entered the judiciary, and rose to the functions of a judge at Göttingen. In 1855 the city of Aurich elected him to the second Chamber of the Hanover Legislature. To accept a legislative or elective office, according to the laws of Hanover, a person in the employ of the government required the permission of the crown. The "crown" of Hanover at that time sat upon the forehead of poor old, blind, stupid King George; and King George refused Bennigsen the indispensable consent. There was but one alternative, and Bennigsen adopted it. He could not be a judge and a deputy, but he could be a deputy by ceasing to be a judge. He promptly resigned his judgeship and with it all hopes of preferment under the government, and, as a free man, took his seat in the parliament.

At Göttingen the young jurist had formed acquaintances which were eventful for him, and which have been not uneventful for the history of Germany. Two of these, Zachariœ and Miguel, were his fellow-students and fellow-legislators; and one of them, Miguel, has been his inseparable companion and faithful ally in all his labors for unity. On entering the parliament in 1866, Bennigsen at once took a position as leader of the opposition. The government was in the hands of the notorious Count Harries. He was a reactionist of the most extreme character, and the King was completely in his power. The Court was full of his creatures; and was almost equally notorious for the profligate adventurers who shut out every sign of Liberalism, and the covetous priests who took care of the King's conscience to the scandal of true religion. Against the sway of this corrupt and demoralizing clique, Bennigsen waged a gallant but hopeless fight down to the year 1866. It needed the soldiers of Prussia to drive them away, and to accomplish with the iron hand what political methods had failed to effect.

In 1859 Bennigsen and Miguel, with a few others, drew up and issued a programme or scheme of German unity. It was a document which made a profound effect throughout the country. The liberalism and patriotism of the Fatherland were either wasting their forces in hopeless contests with reaction, as in Prussia and Hanover itself; or were patching up at Frankfort the wrecks of frail confederations ; or were hiding, crushed and cowed, before the police. Bennigsen's appeal was addressed to an earnest but bewildered public; it was answered with enthusiasm and joy.

The programme embraced a scheme of construction and a scheme of action. In the former the author, Hanoverian as he was, distinctly threw Austria overboard, and declared that only Prussia could be at the head of an united Germany. He proposed to intrust the executive power to the crown of Prussia, while the legislative power should be in the hands of a National German Parliament elected by universal suffrage. What Bismarck has actually accomplished, this leader advocated twenty years ago. If this were his only merit, perhaps too much stress ought not to be laid upon it. A great many other men saw and defended the necessity of a national legislature in those days ; and a parliament of Frankfort, thinking it had reconstructed the German Empire, once offered the imperial dignity to King Frederic Wilhelm of Prussia. It was not so much the prescience of Bennigsen in finding the basis of a solid union, as the practical skill in organizing public sentiment in favor of this basis, that is his great merit.

I have already spoken of the object of the *National-Verein*, and its relation to German politics. It held its first meeting in accordance with an invitation of Bennigsen, on September 16, 1859, and he himself was properly chosen President. Among other prominent members were Feodor Streit, Fries of Weimar, Schulze-Delitsch, Unruh, Loewe, Miquel. The Frankfort Assembly formed the permanent organization of the *National-Verein* and fixed its seat at the city of Coburg. It was prosperous beyond expectation. At the time of its dissolution in 1866 it numbered thirty thousand members, of whom ten thousand were from Prussia. In 1866, after the organization of the North German Confederation, making inevitable the speedy realization of the Empire, the union had no further *raison d'être*, and was dissolved. Bennigsen himself, who, by the annexation of Hanover, was made a Prussian, became a member both of the Prussian Lower Chamber and of the North German *Reichstag*.

When the war of 1866 became imminent, Herr von Bennigsen tried, as Prince Hohenlohe tried in Bavaria, to save his country from the folly and certain failure of the Austrian alliance. If the Bavarians were drawn to Austria by the claim of geographical proximity and family ties, the Hanoverians were drawn away from the Prussians by difference of religion and traditional rivalry. The task of the one statesman was therefore as hard as that of the other. But the consequences of failure were not equally disastrous. For while Bavaria suffered only the shame of espousing a losing cause, and a few years of anxiety from 1866 to 1870, Hanover expiated her crime by entering at once into the Prussian commonwealth, and giving up her character as an independent State. It is now the province of Hanover. It is governed from Berlin, like the most ancient part of the Prussian domains, and for the loss of a blind king it enjoys the presence of Prince Albert of Prussia, a nephew of King William. All this occurred doubtless quite as much according to the wishes as the predictions of Bennigsen.

It has been explained in previous articles how the reconciliation was effected in 1866. The government, which had organized its army, and fought the war in spite of the adverse votes of the Chamber, came forward after the battle of Sadowa and asked for a vote of indemnity, which the majority, carried away by enthusiasm over the victory, promptly conceded. This involved, necessarily, a readjustment of party relations. Out of the progressive party and the more moderate conservatives was founded the National Liberal party, and of this one of the leading spirits was Herr von Bennigsen. It is now the most powerful of all the parliamentary and political factions in Germany, and is practically, though not avowedly, the Government party. Although not stronger than all the other factions together, it can generally elect the parliamentary officers, and by judicious leagues organize a parliamentary majority.

During the war of 1870 Bennigsen was in confidential relations with the Prussian authorities, and undertook, in the interest of the common cause, two important missions. The one was to the South German States, where he discussed the conditions of a possible unity. The other was to the camp at Versailles in the winter of 1871, where the same negotiations were afterwards carried out to a practical result. He is much esteemed by the Government of Prussia, not less for his sterling qualities as a patriot than for his practical and unpretending business capacity.

The reputation which Bennigsen had won as President of the *National-Verein* caused his selection in 1873 as President of the Prussian House of Deputies. Herr von Forckenbeck had, for several years, presided over that body, but in 1873 he was appointed to the "*Herrenhaus*" on the nomination of his native city, Breslau, and Bennigsen almost by acclamation was made his successor. He is a capable and popular presiding officer. Less elastic and nervous in manner than Forckenbeck, less venerable and impressive in appearance than Simson, he strikes the spectator as a practical, well-informed parliamentarian, with strong opinions judicially subordinated to the duties of his position. In the *Reichstag* he may be found sharing with Dr. Simson the two seats which the majority reserves for its most honored members. As a private legislator he can, of course, in the Imperial Parliament throw off the reserve imposed on him in the Prussian House. He is not a frequent speaker. He does not enter much into the ordinary play of debate, the interrogatory, the interruption, the retort, and what may be called the skirmishing that precedes great parliamentary battles. But when the columns of infantry close he is an effective leader. He is a close and cogent reasoner, but is not without the fire and emphasis of an orator. As he is less radical and adventurous than Lasker, and generally defends views not far removed from those of the Wilhelmstrasse, he is heard with a marked but somewhat patronizing respect by Prince Bismarck.

The particular significance of Bennigsen for political observers lies, however, not more in the past or the present than in the possibilities of the future. He is what is called an available man. He has many friends and no enemies, he enjoys the support of his party and the confidence of the government, and the hopes of his friends do not end at the presidency of the House of Deputies. The hopes of a man's friends are not always an accurate measure of his prospects. But Bennigsen is a thoroughly self-reliant man; and it is as clear on the one hand that he has never been pushed forward beyond his merits, as on the other that he has proved equal to every position in which he has been placed. Hence they who claim for him the succession to Prince Bismarck, do not trespass on the domain of the impossible. Their calculation may be premature, and they do not, perhaps, take account of all the influences and considerations that will govern the choice of the next *Reichskanzler*, but there are no infallible reasons for excluding Bennigsen. The circumstances of the time would count for quite as much as the claims of the rival candidates. If the Chancellorship becomes vacant during the reign of the present Emperor, he may declare that he has coquetted long enough with Liberalism, and prefer to close his régime under the ministry of a politician of the old school, full of respect for the traditions of the past. If, however, a new Emperor, be at the head of affairs, disposed by a moderate policy to conciliate the esteem of the great Liberal majority, he will probably select some parliamentary leader who enjoys influence and respect among his colleagues and authority in the country at large. No man answers this description better than Rudolph von Bennigsen.

VIII.

DR. SIMSON.

HERR BRACHVOGEL takes Dr. Simson as the typical representative of parliamentary life in Germany. "The year 1848," he says, "was the mother of German parliamentarism, as well as the cradle of the capacity which Dr. Martin Eduard Simson has developed in political life." Only a remarkable year, even in Germany, the reader will observe, could be at once a mother and a cradle. "Simson," pursues his biographer, "and parliamentarism"—I continue to use the indispensable word, for which there is logical and analogical, if not etymological, authority—"Simson and parliamentarism, or the legal participation of the German States in their own and in the general German political life, are quite inseparable. Our jurist, distinguished as he is in his profession, would hardly have excited and retained in so high a degree the public attention, would hardly have become so important a factor in our political life, if he had not entered so early and so successfully the parliamentary domain. Therefore, both must be painted together, especially because the stages of development through which he has passed, are those of the most of his colleagues, in fact of parliamentarism in Germany."*

Dr. Simson was born on the 10th of November, 1810, in Königsberg, a city which has produced perhaps more than its share of the modern liberal spirits of Germany. His early education was conducted there, and his early studies in jurisprudence, at the university of the same city. Afterwards he was at Berlin and Bonn, and heard the lectures of Niebuhr, the great historian, and Savigny, the great jurist. In 1829, he received his degree of *Doctor Juris*. Soon after the July Revolution, he undertook, on the advice of Niebuhr, a journey to Paris. Herr Brachvogel indulges in some fanciful reflections upon the possible influence exercised on the young jurist by the government of the "citizen king." It may have tended to confirm in him the sentiments of moderate liberalism by which he has always been distinguished. On returning, he chose an academical career, and settled in his native city, as tutor (*Docent*) of Roman law. This was in 1831. In 1833, he became extraordinary, in 1835, regular professor. In 1834, he had become a member of the so-called "Tribunal for the Kingdom of Prussia." In 1845, he was secretary of the commission on the revision of East-Prussian provincial law, and, a year later, he was made *Tribunalrath*. In 1847, he traveled in England, and studied the institutions of the jury and the justice of the peace, as well as the

---

* Brachvogel, *Die Männer der neuen deutschen Zeit.* Vol. III., p. 393.

English constitution in general. The year 1848 came. One of the first whom it brought into prominence was this jurist, who was at once a scholar and a man of the world; whose mind had been not only enriched by study, but also enlarged by travel and observation, who was in the prime of life, and in the possession of all the avenues to popular esteem.

At this epoch, Herr Brachvogel distinguishes four prominent factions in political life. 1st. That which demanded freedom, and nothing further. This was made up of the republicans, the radicals, and the socialists. 2d. That which demanded first freedom and then unity. This was the constitutional party, the liberals, the great majority of the nation. 3d. That which demanded first unity and then freedom. This was the great *Reichspartei*. 4th. That which demanded unity and nothing further. This was composed of the friends of an hereditary German Empire, the royalists, the absolutists, the reactionists.

This classification, without being infallible, is sufficiently accurate to serve as a convenient key to subsequent complications. Dr. Simson belonged vaguely to the third of these factions. He believed, indeed, in freedom, but he also believed that it was conditional on unity, and that patriotism and statesmanship alike dictated that the first be the original object. In Prussia, at this time, the liberals were trying through their constituent assembly to secure unity through freedom. At Frankfort, in the German National Assembly, they were trying to effect freedom through unity. Simson naturally sympathized with the latter, and Königsberg made him a member. Here he belonged to the moderate Right, the so-called "Casino" party, which carried him to the secretaryship, and in September, the same year, made him vice-president. In the middle of December the president of the Assembly was called into the ministry, and Simson became his successor. At each following monthly election he was re-elected, till May, when ill-health compelled him to resign. On April 3, 1849, he was at the head of the deputation which, in behalf of the Frankfort Parliament, went to Berlin to offer the German Imperial crown to Frederic William IV., and received from him the answer: "The German Imperial crown will only be won on the field of battle."

On recovering his health, Dr. Simson did not resume his mission at Frankfort, but with Heinrich von Gogern and a few other liberals of the same school, founded an association at Gotha. They were called in derision, "The Gothaer," and their well-meant scheme proved a general failure. It defended the so-called "triple league of kings"—a temporary alliance formed between Prusssia, Saxony, and Hanover. In 1850, Dr. Simson entered the second chamber of the Prussian Parliament, and became leader of the opposition. The ministry of Manteuffel was in power, and had first signalized itself by the famous humiliation of Olmütz.

The chamber at that time contained three leading factions. On the left sat the extreme radicals of all classes, who with a good deal of rough unmanageable talent, numbered also a few men of high culture and fearless political steadfastness, such as Jacoby, Struve, Loewe, Brentano, and Waldeck. On the opposite side, the right, were seated the conservatives, divided into two groups, the Catholics, and the old Protestants. In the center sat the constitutional, or liberal party, whose leaders were Schwerin, Forckenbeck, Unruh, Grabow, and Simson.

Dr. Simson retained his seat only one year. The state of parliamentary life at that time does not seem to have pleased him. There prevailed an uninterrupted warfare between the chamber and the ministry, or between the successive chambers and the different ministries; and the futile efforts from year to year to effect compromises only made matters worse. 'If the ministers were stubborn and despotic, and persisted in ignoring the principles, while they admitted the fact of constitutional government, it must be said, on the other hand, that the opposition was often unreasonable and intemperate, and prevented harmony by the extravagance of its demands. Extravagant, I mean, not in a theoretical sense, but in a practical sense.

It is impossible to question the perfect soundness of the general principles maintained by Jacoby and Waldeck, but they made the practical mistake of trying to lift an absolute monarch and a monarchical people, at once, to the height of English or American liberty. Dr. Simson could be the champion neither of ministers who persistently denied the House the respect guaranteed by the Constitution, nor of radicals who maintained the exclusive authority of Parliament. He sat neither with the servile right, nor with the irreconcilable left. He was of the moderate or constitutional party, but in those times there was but little for him or it to do. The battle was between the extremes. The moderates held really the balance of power, but they were unpracticed in parliamentary life, and seldom knew how to use their position to advantage. Dr. Simson returned, therefore, to Königsberg and resumed his pedagogic and judicial functions.

This lasted till 1860. In that year he was again sent to the second Chamber of the Prussian *Landtag*, and acted one year as its president. Although the majority of the House belonged to the radical wing of the Liberals, while Dr. Simson was classed with the moderate or *Alt-Liberalen*, the general respect for his integrity as a man, and his capacity as a parliamentarian, secured his election over a stricter partisan. The year of his presidency was remarkable for the uninterrupted conflict of the majority with the War Minister von Roon. He represented at once the soldier's contempt for the civil powers, and the aristocrat's contempt for parliamentary forms. The records of those days are full of his despotic and insolent utterances to the representatives of the people of Prussia, but it must be said that the majority did not always show itself conciliatory and reasonable. Dr. Simson, as a strict parliamentarian, tried to maintain justice between the enraged parties. No complaint of injustice has been specifically formulated, and he retained throughout the respect of all. But after the new House met, in 1862, the majority preferred a more pronounced radical for president, and the choice fell upon Grabow.

I agree fully with Herr Brachvogel that Dr. Simson is the best typical representative of parliamentary life in Germany. His claim to that distinction does not rest alone on the number of assemblies over which he has presided; nor does the respect paid by public opinion to his eminent fitness for such labors, constitute alone his claim to that distinction. The very character of the man, so far as that can be compared to the character or elements of an institution, corresponds to parliamentary life in his own country. I do not speak of the stormy transition period in Prussia, up to 1865, with which Dr. Simson could have had but little sympathy. A calm, conciliatory, moderate man, his conception of a model legislature is that of one in which serious, thoughtful patriots meet for deliberation, one from which violent passions and extreme opinions are alike excluded, and which strives to march in harmony with all the other elements of public life. And this I believe to be the prevailing view throughout the country. It must be remembered that the earliest Prussian Parliaments issued from exceptional circumstances. Coming into being as the fulfillment of a promise long broken by the crown, and through a constitution not deliberately adopted by the people, but *granted* by the king on the eve of an unsuccessful insurrection, and confronted by ministers who openly acknowledged no authority but that of their sovereign, those assemblies naturally reflected all the anger and discontent of a people deceived. They seem more radical in feeling by contrast with the aggressive reaction in the government, and they were driven to extreme acts by the arrogance and folly of their foe. But that these were momentary phenomena and not abiding characteristics, is shown by the subsequent course of events. The composition of the present House of Deputies is not essentially different from that of those days. The same elements, indeed the same men, are to-day in control. But the exasperating Jacobinism of the past decade has given way to a moderation which approaches timidity ; and the leaders, whose noisy dissent used to drive ministers out of the

House, are now the bulwarks of a mild conservatism. The course of events has changed the forms but not the principles of their parliamentary action. In other words, it has brought them nearer to the system of belief and line of policy of Dr. Simson.

If ever English political life and methods were to be introduced into Germany, Dr. Simson would be their chosen representative. He looks the English gentleman as exactly as he acts him. He is a man of medium height, with a smooth, refined face, the soft gray whiskers and the clear, mild, benevolent eyes of a gentleman of the old school. Of English statesmen he most resembles Sir Roundell Palmer, or, as he is now, Lord Selborne; and of Americans, the late Senator Buckingham, of Connecticut. He looks like a man in whom respect for order, for authority, for the amenities of political life were predominant. The sharp irony, the bitter retort, would seem out of place on his life. In a system where the courtesies of life counted for more than the conquests, where personal honor was as sacred as written laws, where a sober conservatism and respectable mediocrity gave the prevailing tone, Dr. Simson would hold and deserve a high rank.

In 1862 came Bismarck, and the conflict resumed the intensity which could only precede its end. During the interval from that time to 1866, when the "reconciliation" completely changed the relations of existing parties, Dr. Simson sat as a private member of the House and accepted no more prominent position than that of President of the Committee on Justice, or, as we would say, "Chairman of the Judiciary Committee." The reconciliation was almost a vindication of his political method. Royer Collard said,

La France est Centre Gauche, meaning that the real opinions of the country were moderately liberal ; and Guizot, the great exponent of *bourgeois* government, said that the true seat of parliamentary power was in the two centers. Dr. Simson is the model *bourgeois* legislator. Equally removed from the reactionary obstinacy of the ministers and the intolerant radicalism of the majority, he had always believed that a safe compromise, inspired by a common prudence and effected by mutual concession, was sure to be finally effected. The country did not share his opinions. It had been firmly believed that the combat between Bismarck and the Landtag was one *à outrance.* It could only end in the complete triumph of the parliamentary principle, or a victory of the ministry and a return to mediæval systems.

Events proved that Dr. Simson was right. The compromise effected after the Austrian war, or rather the reconciliation, modified the temper and the pretensions of both parties to the long strife, and out of the fiery furnace issued the relations which are now at the bottom of parliamentary institutions, both national and imperial.

Dr. Simson became again indispensable. The North German Confederation followed the battle of Sadowa, and the first German Parliament introduced a new legislative factor. It met for the first time in February, 1867, and Dr. Simson was elected president almost by acclamation. In October of the same year, he was at the head of a commission which presented to the king an address voted by the *Reichstag.* In 1870, as President of the *Reichstag,* he was at the head of a deputation which went to Versailles to greet the King of Prussia, or German Emperor. On the constitution of the Imperial Parliament, Dr. Simson was again made president and remained such until 1874. Ill health forced him to relinquish a post of so much labor, and to abandon a sort of work which had occupied him for nearly twenty-five years. He did not, however, surrender his seat as a deputy.

Here we leave the subject of the sketch, sitting in the *Reichstag*, in which he has almost a paternal interest, and enjoying the esteem and confidence of the whole country. At his age, no new field of political activity is likely to open for him. But, if ever an emergency arises for which the country requires a man who unites firmness of conviction with moderation of temper, who enjoys an authority won by long years of faithful service, and whose personal character has never been stained even by slander, many eyes will be at once directed to Martin Eduard Simson.

PART V.

THE PARTY LEADERS.

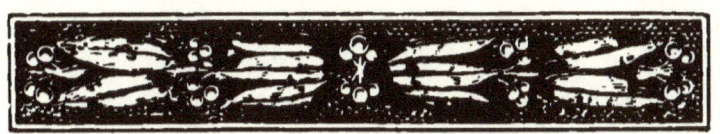

IX.

EDUARD LASKER.

THIS gentleman introduces us to a new e'ement in German political life. Hitherto we have treated only of the statesman in office, in charge of a portfolio, or at the head of an embassy, or scolding reluctant deputies from the president's chair; now we come to the delegates of the people, who owe nothing to the favor of princes, and who are the less admired at court the more they are admired throughout the country. Numbers of these men have arisen even within the short life of Prussian and German constitutionalism. Some of them have passed forever from the scene of political warfare; others, still living, have been swept to the rear by the changing current of affairs; a few still retain and wield the authority won in past decades. I have taken five men who represent, if not five distinct parties, at least five distinct currents or forms of political action. One stands for the National Liberal party, the majority in the Imperial Parliament, and the party of the great middle class of Germany. A second stands for the *Fortschritts-partei*, the party of progress, composed of the uncompromising radicals who respect abstract principles. A third is the champion of the Ultramontane faction, the only regular opposition. A fourth represents that sort of political radicalism in which the theories of social and industrial reform predominate. Finally, the fifth is political radicalism, pure, fearless, and irreconcilable.

The first of these characters, and to-day the one best known, is Eduard Lasker. He is the natural and the accepted leader of the National Liberals; and to this honor, which he has won by his own talents, the favor of the crown has never added that of an administrative office. A tribune of the people he has always been, and will doubtless remain. If Bismarck is the powerful minister, strong in the force of his own character, in the support of the King, and in the affections of a reunited people, Lasker is the private deputy whose consummate ability the government is obliged to respect, and whose unselfish devotion to liberal principles the people are glad to acknowledge. If Prince Hohenlohe, the scion of a house which had done homage to Frederick Barbarossa, has won a high rank in a profession which has always shared with the army the favor of the aristocracy, Lasker has won an influence on domestic legislation quite unparalleled in Germany. If Simson and Bennigsen are satisfied to preside over deliberations that they cannot direct, Lasker, refusing any distinction which he had not earned, would likewise refuse any distinction not accompanied by power. He is the leading Commoner of Prussia, just as Waldeck was twenty years ago. The difference is that Waldeck was a radical leader in the days when Prussia was slowly fighting her way to a settled constitutional system, while Lasker is the leader of an established majority not only in Prussia, but in the more spacious arena of German politics.

The official record of his career, as given in the parliamentary almanacs, is, up to a certain point, not unlike that of the great body of German barristers. He was born in Berlin on the 14th of October, 1829, a Jew. After a preliminary course at the Elizabeth Gymnasium in Breslau, he entered the university of the same city, in 1847, and graduated a doctor of laws in 1851. He then became *pro formâ* an *Auscultator* at the Municipal Court of Berlin. Soon afterwards he removed to England, where he lived two or three years. The compiler of the almanac does not state the object of this voluntary exile; but I believe that it was the young advocate's intention to make England his permanent home, and to pursue there, under more favorable advantages, his chosen profession. Be that as it may, his plans were subsequently changed. In 1856, he reappeared in Berlin and passed the next stage of his judicial career, that of *Assessor*. In 1870, he abandoned the bench and resumed the practice of the law as an advocate. He was first elected to the House of Deputies from the 4th Berlin district, in 1865, and was re-elected in 1866. Up to the battle of Sadowa, he had been classed with the advanced Liberals; but after that event and the modified situation which followed, he abandoned his old associates and aided to found the National Liberal party. In the North German Confederation he was a member of the Constituent *Reichstag*, and of the subsequent legislative *Reichstags*. When the Empire was organized and an Imperial

Reichstag—no tautology will be detected here by people who know that the German word *Reich* does not designate a form of government—was elected, Lasker was the successful candidate in half-a-dozen districts, and accepted the election for the second district in the Duchy of Saxe-Meiningen. In the Prussian *Landtag*, he now sits for Frankfort on the Main. Aside from parliamentary work, he is solicitor of the " Deutsche Baden-Credit Bank," or, *Crédit Foncier*.

These outlines of Lasker's life afford abundant subject for reflection. It would be interesting to trace the probable reasoning which led the young advocate to abandon his native land and all hopes of preferment among his own people; and it could doubtless be found that, like so many of his countrymen, he saw at that time very little promise of a real constitutionalism, under which merit alone should prevail. It would be curious to speculate on the result for him and England, if he had not returned to Germany. The position which he has acquired in Germany would hardly have been opened to him in England. Political prejudice may not be so strong there as in Germany, but social prejudices are far stronger; and the race which in the latter country has fought its way upward in art, literature, in legislation, in every field where genius prevails, has in English politics but one striking representative, and he has not retained the faith. But for that, the tremendous social opposition which he met, would perhaps have mastered him. Lasker is far honester than Disraeli. He has clung to his original Hebrew faith in spite of all the advantages which apostasy offered to an ambitious man, and his political integrity is out of the reach of slander. His virtues would perhaps have been respected, but in private life, by the English. If he had remained in London, he would have learned to pronounce English with a strong accent of which he himself would have been delightfully unconscious; he would have become a clever little attorney with a good run of petty cases, especially among his fellow emigrants; and in his leisure, he would have written elegant correspondence for German journals and reviews. But the German Parliament would have lost in him a legislator of splendid and sustained abilities, and the German youth the example of a patriot who is a statesman from a sense of duty, of a citizen above reproach.

Again, one may draw with tolerable accuracy the outlines of such a judicial career as Lasker, with the indispensable encouragement, might have pursued. The indispensable encouragement was that of the crown or of the authorities who represented the crown. But the authorities of those days were devoted conservatives, and they won the favor of a king who professed just motives of conduct, by distributing his bounty with a jealous care for the interests of altar and throne. Lasker could claim no special sympathy with those interests. He had indeed sworn a formal allegiance to his sovereign, but he was a strong liberal and, in the jargon of the "Wilhelmstrasse," liberalism then meant disloyalty. He was the subject of a Christian king, but the constitution permitted him formally to adhere to his native faith. A radical and a Jew, he united in himself the two most formidable barriers to professional preferment. For twelve years, from 1858 to 1870, he filled the humble, unsalaried post of *assessor* at the Berlin Municipal Court, and retired after the experience that there was no opening in the judiciary for him. During that time, he had seen promoted over his head armies of young candidates in the same service. They wanted his ability, it is true, and his courage, and his independence, and nearly all the qualities which dignify manhood, but they were brilliant defenders of the conservative interests of society, and, above all, of that form of conservative interests which had been intrusted to the royal ministry of Justice. Nor did they hide their light under a bushel. They fearfully extolled from the bench the beneficence of the existing reign, they boldly vindicated their official superiors in the evening club at the beer-house. Lasker was more timid, or perhaps less servile. Regarding his position as one which he had a right, as a Prussian subject, to claim, and demanding a promotion which was justified by his great talents, he would not purchase favor by the prostitution either of his office or his opinions. He did not indeed shrink from expressing such opinions as he conscientiously held and might legally publish. In the political clubs he was known as a brilliant and captivating radical orator, in periodicals his graceful pen discussed the pressing questions of the day. But this temerity was, of course, fatal to him. The more he spoke and wrote, the less favorable became his hopes of professional success.

At the same time, this invidious partiality may have been a real, though disguised, blessing. Lasker the judge would have excluded Lasker the parliamentary leader, and the history of Prussia and Germany might have been other than what it is. If he had been a sound reactionist and had had aristocratic connections, when he began his legal career twenty years ago, he would have enjoyed every promotion through the several stages of an advocate's career;

would have found an early entrance into the judiciary, and would now have a high position on the bench and a good salary. But, in that case, he would have been only a wheel in the mechanism of the State, whereas Providence had reserved him for a higher destiny.

Coming into public life, or, at least into prominence, at the close of the *Conflikts-Zeit*, Lasker enjoys the advantage of freedom from the still glowing animosities of that period. His first election, as stated above, was in the year 1865. He then belonged to the "Party of Progress," which had united in opposition to the reactionary policy of the ministry all the undaunted liberal spirits; but, obeying scruples of modesty, if no others, he did not at once take a prominent part in the debate. While Sadowa was fought, Lasker watched the battle as a silent member. After Sadowa had been fought and won, party relations were changed; and it may be said that Lasker's parliamentary career began first with the reconciliation made in 1866, and the new era ushered in by that famous transaction.

Not an inaccurate theory of Lasker's parliamentary position even at that time, that is to say after he became leader of the National Liberal party, is hinted at in the last number of the *Grenzboten*: "The greater part of the National Liberal party," says the writer, "is liberal conservative; yet the party is generally led by some men of great talents, of whom the majority ought, according to their political principles, to lead the party of progress." The liberal party certainly counts many other able men, some of whom bear, perhaps, with impatience the sway of a young Hebrew lawyer. Some of these have already been or will be treated in this volume. Such, for instance, are Heinrich von

Treitschke, who had a reputation as a historical student and a graceful writer, long before he became a politician, and who is one of the staunchest and healthiest of Liberals; Bennigsen, who has at least paternal claim on the leadership; and Dr. Simson, who enjoys the respect of all parties. There is furthermore Max von Forckenbeck, the successor of Simson and present Speaker of the *Reichstag*, a Liberal, although a nominal Roman Catholic, Burgomaster of the City of Breslau, in Silesia, and one of the younger politicians of Prussia. He has made himself familiar with the duties of his place, and enjoys the support of the whole House; but he lacks a good voice and a dignified manner, which our prejudices exact of the speaker of such an assembly. Louis Bamberger, one of the exiles of 1848, is a practical banker, and speaks frequently on financial questions; Carl Braun, a journalist and advocate, is a clever and popular speaker on general subjects; Schulte is active in the ecclesiastical conflict; Heinrich Oppenheim is another authority on economical topics; and there are many others whose absence from these pages implies no indifference to their merits. But none of these can dispute with Lasker the leadership of the majority. He is not only the leader by virtue of superior talents which always assert themselves, but in consequence of a formal choice by the party itself. He is its forensic organ; he announces in Parliament its resolutions; and, when necessary, he sustains them by all the force of his eloquence.

I have spoken of Lasker's oratorical abilities, but it would be more just to call him the first of German debaters. His parliamentary efforts have more of the English practical, realistic character, and less of the art and method of France or America. One searches in vain through Lasker's speeches, and, indeed, through the entire literature of Germany, for such symmetrical and finished specimens of oratorical art as those of the great French divines, of Berryer and the masters of French form, or of the famous orators of the United States. It does not lie in the genius of the German people, much less in that of Lasker himself. He wants many qualities which are almost essential to a great orator. He has neither an imposing figure, nor a dignified presence, nor a sonorous voice. He is about as small as Earl Russell; and, although a man of more natural talent, he has never held, like the former, positions which bring responsibility and authority. He is the delight of the Berlin *gamins*, the pet of the comic press. He is the parliamentary Puck, and one expects him to burst forth:

> "Up and down, up and down,
> I will lead them up and down:
> I am feared in field and town;
> Goblin, lead them up and down."

He would be an admirable prime minister in the kingdom of Lilliput. In spite of the solemnity of his manner, he seems always to be an escaped member of some fairy band,—an elf or sprite,—and it would be thought the most natural thing in the world, if he should be seen scampering over the top of the desks, kicking over the inkstands of grave deputies, and pulling their shaggy beards. The other short men of the *Reichstag* do not cause such an impression. Delbrück is also very short, but he never impresses as being unusually, much less ludicrously, so. Windthorst, the ultramontane leader, is very small, but his manner is so aggressive, and his wit so ferocious, that in hearing him speak one adds several feet to his stature. Lasker, on the other hand, is the most earnest man in the House, but the contrast with his size always ends in a sense of the ludicrous. The solemnity is more absurd because unexpected. If Lasker were more sprightly, he would not so often suggest the sprite. If he had more wit, he would excite less laughter.

His voice is high and, notwithstanding a slight lisp, very clear. Few speakers make themselves heard more easily, not only in the Prussian House of Deputies, but also against the wretched acoustics of the *Reichstag ;* and few could throw so much emphasis into so modest an organ. These merits he owes in great part to his singular articulation. Higginson has said that an essay of Emerson is like a string of pearls, because the sentences may be told off, one by one, each complete in itself. The same description may be applied to the articulation of Lasker. The words drop from his tongue, clear and sharp, like the ticking of a rapid pendulum; and he has a habit of accumulating speed as he moves through a sentence till the end, when he lets his voice drop plumply on the last word, and begins again. It is somewhat mechanical, and even monotonous, but very effective in debate. His fluency is of that perfect kind, which is not simply command of words, but which never wants for sentences or thoughts. His speeches sound like perpetual perorations. One expects that each sentence is the culmination. While this feature, by deceiving the patience of hearers, secures their unbroken attention, it mars the effect of a discourse as a work of art, and, with increased familiarity, becomes a tedious mannerism. Unfortunately, Lasker, like many other fluent and ready speakers, is not sufficiently sparing of his gifts. His position as spokesman of the National Liberal party gives him, of course, great authority, and his ability and earnestness give him still more; but his oratory has not improved during the past year or two, and many people believe that his power over an audience is on the wane.

Several of Lasker's public or parliamentary efforts have attained the rank of historical events. One of these was a eulogy delivered at the grave of his friend and Liberal colleague, Twesten. Lasker, as has been explained, is a zealous and uncompromising Jew, and Twesten, though a Liberal and a member of the party which the former led, was an equally steadfast Protestant; but this did not prevent Lasker from saying, at the tomb of his friend, words which were acceptable to both Hebrew and Christian. The discourse was printed and obtained a wide circulation. It was more artistically constructed than his parliamentary speeches; and while it revealed a good command of the resources of rhetoric, and a finely trained critical faculty, it was not without those more feeling passages which disclose the emotion of a bereaved friend.

Lasker's most memorable parliamentary triumph was probably the exposure of what is known as the Northern Railway scandal; and the overthrow of the Minister of Commerce, Count Itzenplitz. A few words will explain this achievement, which had a social as well as a political significance. Its social significance lay in the fact that it was the triumph of an honest, radical Jew over speculating, Christian aristocrats; its political significance, in the fact that parliamentary pressure, supported by public indignation, was able to expel a favorite minister of the king. If there was one thing more than another which confirmed the aversion of the Prussian aristocracy to commercial occupations, it was the theory, which was by no means unsupported by facts, that they were the chosen domain of the Israelites. This was especially true of that large class of financial enterprises which involve elements of risk, and in which a striking audacity,—hovering along the borders of that region where the daring becomes the dishonest—the speculator, the swindler,—is even more important, as a source of power, than capital and patience. Even when individual nobles, driven by necessity or some higher cause, entered upon a career of trade and sent their ships abroad over the seas, like Antonio, it was a tradition that they always fell a prey to the Shylock of their time and country. It is not worth while to dispute about what was cause and what effect, whether the aristocracy shrank from business because it was in the hands of Jews, or the Jews usurped the field because it was neglected by the aristocracy. That is perhaps a question, but the fact itself is clear enough. The Spaniard Quevedo, whenever he heard of a quarrel between two men, always asked: "Who is the woman?" In Germany, when a startling commercial scheme became known, or an imposing swindle was revealed, the country gentlemen asked, "Is his name Isaac, or Jacob, or Moses?"

One may easily believe that it was not less a pleasure than a duty for Lasker to show the other side of this picture. During the session of 1873, he made a speech on the budget, in which he declared that a regular system of fraud was in operation in the ministry of commerce, by which certain persons were using their official position to make themselves rich. He specified two men, both of aristocratic blood and connections, and one a great favorite of Prince Bismarck himself. The latter was a sub-official in the ministry of commerce; and Lasker charged that he had granted or promised the granting of railway concessions with an over prudent regard for the interests of himself and his friends. He demanded a parliamentary investigation. It happened that honest and reactionary old General von Roon was, at that time, playing the comedy of minister-president, and he resented this assault upon the flower of Prussian Junkerdom. In answer to Lasker's speech, he promised, indeed, to have the matter examined, but with rare temerity he pronounced the charges false. Lasker accepted this challenge. In two long and masterly speeches which were exhaustive accounts of the railways at issue, and which were full of the most astounding revelations, he not only persuaded the House to grant the desired investigation, but he even convinced von Roon himself that the charges were true. The latter was frank enough to rise and say that if he had known the facts before, he would never have made the statement that he made. The investigation by a mixed commission, appointed by the government and the House, was accordingly held. The result was that the inculpated official was dismissed; and the minister of commerce, whose negligence and inefficiency had proved so costly, was forced by public opinion to retire.

A year later the liberal leader arraigned another illustrious personage, Prince Putbus. He also had built railways, and, according to Lasker, had been guilty of practices which revealed genius indeed, but a species of genius which by rigid moralists is looked on with disfavor. Putbus was very angry. His aristocratic blood boiled at this interference of an heterodox plebeian with his financial operations, and he demanded a military court of inquiry. He is an officer of the Landwehr, and he asked a court of his comrades to say whether he had done anything unworthy of his honor, as a soldier and a gentleman. This court acquitted him, and the subject dropped.

It is one of the infirmities of human nature that the discovery of sin is a secret pleasure, when the sinners are our enemies; and Eduard Lasker is not above humanity. But if his relations to the alleged swindles did sharpen his reforming zeal, it has not been disputed that the effect of his exposures was wholesome in the highest sense. They tore aside forever the heavy veil of social prejudice, which had so long shielded the deeds of the *noblesse* from the eye of public criticism; and placed the golden rule of integrity on a thoroughly democratic basis. They made Lasker the most popular man in Prussia. He was admired as the great tribune of the people, and loved as warmly as he was admired. Of course, the ministers were annoyed at these uncanonical feats on the part of the leader of the government majority, in Parliament. They could not exactly defend established guilt, nor could they ask His Majesty to countenance these awkward assaults upon the court favorites. They were placed in an embarrassing dilemma, from which they have not yet escaped. But the bold little deputy, who created the dilemma, won fresh parliamentary laurels and the respect of all good citizens.

Of other important events in Lasker's public career, I recall his vindication of parliamentary privilege in the case of a Catholic deputy, who had been arrested by order of the government during the session ; his skillful plea for an imperial bank, which, at first unsuccessful on a question of form, finally won the substance of the cause ; his elaborate and masterly speeches on law reform, the last, and not the least striking, being that of December, 1875, in which he spoke for the majority of the Liberals against the reactionary proposals of the government ; and finally a variety of speeches on the ecclesiastical issue, the only one, perhaps, on which he accepts without reserve the position and views of the ministry. These speeches reveal the most singular relations that have, perhaps, ever bound the leader of a parliamentary majority to a government. If there be any government party in German or Prussian politics it is the National Liberal party. The majority in the *Reichstag*, as in the *Landtag*, are associated with the measures of Prince Bismarck, for unity and against Ultramontanism, and are always referred to as the ministerial party. In the elections the semi-official press always supports the candidates of this party. I remember, a year ago, after the elections for the *Reichstag*, the *Provinzial Correspondenz*, the most authoritative organ of the government, congratulated the country that the center of parliamentary gravity would continue to lie in the National Liberal party. But neither Bismarck himself, nor a single one of his ministerial subordinates, is a member of that party. The minister of war is a strict Conservative. Dr. Falk and the ministers of commerce and of agriculture belong to the Free Conservatives. Camphausen and Delbrück are so-called Old Liberals, and now build a glorious party of their own. And if the ministers have few actual connections with the

National Liberals, these latter, on the other hand, have very little sympathy with the ministers. Under a strict parliamentary government every one of them, except Bismarck himself, would disappear.

As the leader of the Liberals, Lasker is, more than any other, responsible for the attitude of the party. His influence in shaping its extra-parliamentary resolutions is no less marked than his ability in defending those resolutions before Parliament. But since the defense of the party in the majority of cases implies opposition to the measures proposed by the government, and as Lasker is a legislator who never shrinks from the most extreme statement of his views, it follows that, as a nominal friend of the ministry, he must be one of those uncomfortable friends whose benevolent candor is little less dangerous than open hostility. He is the kindly critic who exacts more than the opposition. His support for bills is won only when they have been shorn of all the features that the government most prizes. Hence Prince Bismarck is much better satisfied when the most bitter Ultramontane takes the floor than when this valiant but captious ally tears his schemes into pieces, under pretense of making friendly suggestions.

If Lasker had not become a practical politician, he would have been one of the first of political critics. His published writings are equally marked by elegance of style, keenness of thought, and breadth of scholarship; and long before he won a parliamentary reputation, they were eagerly accepted by the first periodicals of Germany.. He wrote mainly on political and social topics, and one or two volumes of his essays have been collected and published.

X.

HERR WINDTHORST.

WE come now to the defenders of the sacred order in politics, to the champions of the Church against the legislation of the State. They represent the universal spirit of opposition. They have as energetic a hatred of the Old Protestants who hold a mistaken faith, as of the extreme radicals who hold no faith whatever. With them all the results of pure political action, not inspired by the precepts or sanctioned by the consent of the Church, are but unsubstantial dreams; yet this fact, or this conviction, lessens in no degree the vigor and zeal of their resistance. If their kingdom were truly of this world, and its prizes piously to be sought, they could not act their parliamentary parts with a more studied skill.

The Ultramontanes, as a party, share with the National Liberals the debating talent of the country. Three of their members, Mallinckrodt, Reichensperger, and Windthorst, have carried on their side of the ecclesiastical contest with a skill, an audacity, and a persistence which are not the less admirable, because they are exerted in a hopeless cause. The first of these hardy champions has been removed by death from the field of politics. But Hermann von Mallinckrodt is so conspicuous a figure in the modern Parliamentary life of Germany, and his part is so closely connected with the greatest political issue of these days, that even the traditions of his incisive eloquence have a present value. A member of the Catholic aristocracy of Westphalia, he could, perhaps, trace his family connections and his religious heritage back to Saint Boniface himself. In more prosperous times, he was employed in the local administration of the province, just as he was an active supporter of the Government ten years ago, when Bismarck was trying to strangle Liberalism instead of Ultramontanism. After the outbreak of the ecclesiastical conflict, Mallinckrodt was one of the most determined leaders of the Opposition. He was not only a man of broad general culture, but, in certain subjects, such, for instance, as Church history and dogma, he was a profound and accurate scholar, and almost the only Catholic member who could carry the debates up to that elevation. In him Dr. Falk and Professor Gneist found no unworthy foe. In an intellectual sense his speaking was of the very highest sort. He was not a great orator to sway a popular audience, for his manner was cold and unsympathetic; but he knew how to rivet the general attention by the closeness of his logic and terrify his enemies by the power of his sarcasm. His delivery was quite unlike the German type. He was calm, moderate, and full of self-possession; he was familiar with all the little arts of gesticulation and elocution, and his speeches were specimens of polished and masterly invective. In spite of the exasperating effect of his oratory, Mallinckrodt was perhaps more generally respected than any of his Ultramontane colleagues. When he died, not the Catholic press alone paid his memory tribute, but the Liberal journals mourned the loss of a stalwart foe and an accomplished Parliamentary debator. Peter Reichensperger, the second member of this triumvirate, is cast in a different mould. He was a leading jurist and a judge before he became a leader of the "Centre;" and, if that party had not been created by the exigencies of the times, he would have lived and died a consistent servant of the State. Indeed, he has never quite forgotten the jurist in the legislator. In his political views and in his political methods, he is more considerate that his two colleagues. His speeches are carefully prepared, and are concise, lucid, and cogent. As he discusses the Church question in the tone and with the air of a man who conscientiously feels a grievance, instead of making it a text on which to say disagreeable things of adversaries, he is more fairly treated by his associates, and serves his own cause not the less efficiently.

Both these two men must, however, in the order of talents and influence, give way to Louis Windthorst. The biographical sketch of him, which I find in the parliamentary handbook, reads as if written by himself. It is short and unpretentious, and seems to reveal the same contempt for autobiographical arts and opportunities that he shows for shams and pretenders in parliamentary life. It is worth reproducing entire :

"Windthorst, Ludwig, ex-Minister of State in Hanover. Born 17 January, 1812. Roman Catholic. Attended the

'Carolinum' in Osnabrück, and studied in Göttingen and Heidelberg. Was, first, advocate, then syndic and presiding member of the Consistory at Osnabrück; afterwards *Ober-Appellationsrath* in Kalbe; 1851–1853 and 1862–1865, Minister of Justice in Hanover; finally Chief Syndic of the Crown in Kalbe. 1849–66, member of the Assembly of the Estates of the Realm, and in 1851 president of the second Chamber of the same; member of the Constituent and the regular *Reichstag*, and since 1867, of the Prussian House of Deputies; re-elected for the third district of the Province of Hanover."

This is the list of the public positions filled by Windthorst; unfortunately it includes no account of the way in which he has filled them. If it had been written by his great enemy, Bismarck, or his rival, Lasker, the world would have tested their candor and magnanimity by the degree of recognition expressed by them for the extraordinary talents, the unrivalled sagacity of this leader of the Ultramontane faction. But those critical observations which are forbidden to Windthorst's own pen, or by the dignity of a parliamentary annual, may be found and appropriated in other places. Not the least of the merits of this deputy is that of picturesqueness. He imparts variety to the debates, and illuminates them by those sudden elements of the incongruous, the sense of which is said to be the basis of laughter. The cause of picturesqueness himself, he is at the same time a capital subject for picturesque description. Max Ring has, perhaps, not made the most of his subject, and his closing estimate of Windthorst is patronizingly inadequate, but for an evidently hostile critic he is not altogether and wholly unjust.

"If we turn now toward the Centre," he says, "our attention is immediately drawn to one of the most interesting and best known characters of the *Reichstag*. Directly opposite the president's chair, in the first row, buried in thought, sits a plump little man with a bald head, short-sighted, eyes half hid under the arched brows and a peculiar protuberant upper lip, so that, as the phrase goes, his beauty cannot oppress him. But even here the French proverb prevails: *C'est sa laideur qui fait sa beauté;* for a certain spiritual expression lends a singular charm to a physiognomy, so little marked by beauty, especially when in the course of debate the apparently composed, but really active face becomes animated. Then the little brown eyes sparkle, the lifeless lines expand, and an ironical mocking smile plays along the overhanging lip. Suddenly he interrupts the speaker and shouts a sarcastic remark into the assembly, which commonly causes merriment, but sometimes angry murmurs. The curious little man is no other than the 'Pearl of Meppen,' the Deputy Windthorst, formerly a Hanoverian minister of State under King George, at present the leader and head of the 'Centre' party. For a great statesman and orator, which he would gladly be, he wants the force of truth, and warmth of conviction, which carry hearers irresistibly with them. In the place of these he possesses a sharp understanding, piercing wit, and the coolest ruthlessness in battle with his opponents. He suggests the manner of the French fencing-masters, with their sharp elastic blades. Like them, he spies with his quick glances every exposed point of his foe, and strikes lightning-quick, sure as a serpent. Most interesting is the duel, when he is opposed to his special foe Prince Bismarck.

Then his keenness and daring are doubled; his little eyes are fired with malice, and his wit becomes more biting and cutting. In spite of this, however, little Windthorst generally succumbs to the giant blows of the great Bismarck, whom he cannot reach with his French rapier. Still the 'Pearl of Meppen,' is a dangerous antagonist; he has the most extensive connections on all sides and in the highest circles, and in the choice of means obeys the principles of the Jesuits. Now he reaches out his hand to the Alsatians; next is seen arm in arm with the social-aristocrat Sonnemann; again he smiles on the Conservatives and Particularists, then coquets even with the National Liberals and the Progressivists, whenever, in short, there is a chance to create embarrassments for the government and especially the hated chancellor,—a cunning scout, an unwearied partisan, extraordinary in small warfare, but no commander who fights historic battles."*

A writer in the *Grenzboten* Magazine is less complimentary. He says that what has fortified Windthorst in the parliamentary rank that he has won "is the specific nature of his gifts and his capacity. It is known that he prefers short impromptus to long speeches. He hits best thereby the temper of a House which is almost always in a state of mental weariness, and which sighs with a natural longing for the little jokes and the personal incidents that entertain. Hence in a large measure the flood of 'personal remarks,' encouraged by the House itself, after every sharp debate, and hence the eternal 'merriment,' the stereotyped appearance of which in the reports has given rise to so much

---

*Max Ring in the *Gartenlaube*, 1874, page 292.

unfavorable comment in the provinces. . . . . This chronic exhaustion Windthorst beyond all others knows how to humor. His wit is in no wise brilliant, his humor has a sour smack, his shrewdness wants depth of thought and study. Since he only skims off the foam of the day's excitement, without troublesome soundings into its depths, since he neglects the relations of things, and, with the taste of a cultivated natural talent, pries into the relations of persons, he has always material for bad jokes, or piquant allusions. For this a bored audience is always grateful, and by its applause, if often only ironical, places him higher than he deserves."

Neither of these sketches is complete or accurate. If the former, written in an easier style, presents only the outward characteristics of the man, the latter aims at a more careful theory of his intellectual nature, and neglects all other elements. But they agree in denying him the attributes of a statesman, and in degrading him to the rank of a low comedian on the parliamentary stage.

Nothing could be more unjust and more inexact. If the writers had questioned the sincerity of Windthorst's religious fervor; if they had described the recklessness and unscrupulousness of his political methods; if they had represented him as a powerful critic without constructive or organizing talent, they would not have violated truth or propriety. The Hanoverian leader is not a man to whom nature supplied the conditions of a positive faith; he is *der Geist der stets verneint.* He would be the most daring and consistent of skeptics, if his interests had not made him the most faithful of believers. Even his religious professions spring from one form of unbelief. To be a free-thinker requires the exercise of faith in human reason and in most of the results of human inquiry, while, by espousing the Catholic religion, he proclaimed his disbelief in all positive and uninspired knowledge. He is skeptical on all subjects where skepticism requires the greatest contempt for his fellow beings, and is credulous where he is sure of having the fewest imitators. He doubts everything that is true, and believes only what is doubtful. According to the philosophy of Hegel, the *Ego* and the *Non ego* are identical. Windthorst shows by his own example the identity of absolute skepticism and absolute belief. An original spirit of universal dissent has driven him into a Church which exacts as a first condition vows of unqualified assent.

Windthorst is, perhaps, the model Philistine of German politics, but it must be said that, while refusing to concede to his rivals the influence of moral convictions, he never claims them for his own party. Reichensperger and Schorlemer assume the air of indignant martyrs, but Windthorst never. He is too clever to invite the ironical laughter of the Left. He battles with the Centre, not because he believes in Ultramontanism, but because he hates Prince Bismarck and Prussia; and this freedom from the servitude of a virtuous consistency is of vast advantage to him. He is not compelled to assume an attitude of defence when his Church is assailed, and of silence for the rest of the time. Like a soldier of fortune, he roams over the whole world of politics, and grapples with the foe wherever and whenever he meets him. Less successful in the use of studied irony than Mallinckrodt, and far below him in the breadth and elegance of his acquirements, he is superior in running debate, in rapid repartee, and as a parliamentary manager. He carries on for his faction all the details of the battles, argues the technical questions, and in general watches all the side issues that spring up along the way. To this congenial work he brings a fertility of expedient, a ruthlessness of purpose, and a sharpness of wit, which have no rivals in the House. Under the fire of the fiercest attack he lolls sleepily in his seat, but with one eye always open to the chances of a trenchant interruption.

It would be incorrect, moreover, to say with the writers quoted above, that Windthorst has none of the qualities of a statesman. One may be without moral and intellectual convictions, and yet be able to detect the fallacy in any political theory, or the weaknesses of any proposed measures, and to suggest a better theory or measure. This is the case with Windthorst. His mind is acute, but not shallow; his spirit is cynical, but not frivolous. The rapidity of his intellectual processes does not imply that they are careless or incorrect, and it has always seemed to me that his understanding was sure as well as clear. The leader of a feeble minority has, of course, very little chance of impressing his views upon legislation, but Windthorst is a useful legislator. He is a master of parliamentary law and strategy. In fact, he seems to me to possess many qualities of a statesman, with few of his opportunities; and not many of his colleagues, in any part of the *Reichstag*, are by nature or by training his superior.

They who know Windthorst well, say that none of the ferocity which he shows in parliamentary warfare goes over with him into private life. He is a kindly, agreeable, old gentleman, who is much respected for the Spartan simplicity of his tastes, and much admired for the wit and sprightliness of his conversation. The morose air that he has in public, never, indeed, quite forsakes him, but it does not reveal a morose temper or an unfriendly disposition. The sarcasm which is so terrible, like that of Thaddeus Stevens, is part of his professional equipment. He will make a point against some measure by a crushing personal retort upon one of its defenders, and then apologize to the victim that the force of circumstances made necessary a step which had no element of personal unkindness. But he has never, to my knowledge, shown this sort of remorse toward Prince Bismarck,

The Chancellor once did Windthorst the honor publicly to recognize him as his most formidable antagonist, and since that time, the position of the leader of the Ultramontane faction has not been disputed. A few maintain that the unintentional kindness of the prince prejudiced the chances of other foes equally deserving. This charge is unjust to him. The mind of the prince is singularly "objective," and in choosing to single out Windthorst for personal attack, he was only recognizing a concrete fact, a parliamentary phenomenon. Neither the original position of Windthorst, nor his subsequent growth in authority, owes anything to the partial hostility of the Imperial Chancellor.

XI.

DR. LOEWE.

IN a sense which is much more literal than the metaphor would suggest, Dr. Loewe may be called a landmark in German politics. The distance between him and the government to-day is, in a general way, a key to the progress made by the latter during the past thirty years, but is not evidence of a relapse of the former from the principles of his early life. Prince Bismarck has drawn near to him, but he is unchanged. Added years and calmer times may, indeed, have modified the ardor of youth, and brought with them more respect for the practical conditions of reform; but in principle he is the same uncompromising foe of prerogative, of *Junkerism*, of military pretensions; and the same stanch champion of popular rights. He is a radical, but his radicalism does not exclude statesmanship. He is a radical who endured a long persecution at the hands of the government, with the same dignity that he maintains in the enjoyment of its respect; who received his pardon for the offence of a fervid patriotism with the same manly independence that he preserves in the prosperity of a universal affection.

He is a radical in the German sense, which is not at all the American, nor even the English sense. His mind is, perhaps, rather English than either German or American. He might be compared to Mr. Bright in firmness of conviction and purity of purpose, but he is a better scholar and a more practical legislator. He might be compared to Mr. Forster in the solidity of his understanding and the breadth of his sympathies, but he never barters with current opinions. He showed his independence by remaining with the party of Progress, when nearly all of his friends were organizing a governmental National Liberal party. He showed it again two years since, when, against his radical friends, he voted for a military measure that he deemed necessary to the Empire. Thus he is no idle theorist, neglecting practical even if partial reforms, for abstract and useless impossibilities.

Dr. William Loewe was born at Olvenstedt, near Magdeburg, on the 14th of November, 1814. He studied at the Gymnasium of Magdeburg, and further at the University of Halle, where he graduated as doctor of medicine. His first appearance in political life was in that year which called out for the first time so much political talent, the year 1848, and it saw him as delegate to the Frankfort Parliament. He was President of the "German Parliament" after its secession to Stuttgart. Pursued on account of this circumstance, he went into exile, and remained abroad until 1861, when a general amnesty opened the way for him to return. Since then, he has resided at Berlin, and divided his time between the practice of his profession and legislative work. He is a member both of the Prussian House of Deputies and of the *Reichstag*, and was, until this year, when he refused a re-election, first vice-president of the former.

When the military courtiers and the Conservatives of the old reactionary class assert, as they do, that Dr. Loewe is a revolutionary statesman, they have in their own minds and convey to others a clear notion of what they mean. The term "Revolution" in Germany has been adopted into the jargon of the schools. Every philosopher who lectures at a university gives at least one hour each season to the fundamental difference between revolution and reformation, with personal examples drawn, perhaps, from Napoleon and Luther. The former revolutionized without reforming; the latter reformed without revolutionizing. The one was a pernicious disturber of social order; the other was a beneficent, corrective force. The Frenchman pursued the French method; the German, the German method. This is the accepted formula, but its application to the course of events in history is not so simple. Of which of these two processes, for instance, is the existing parliamentary system the result? The discontented Radical, who chafes under military dominion and the fetters imposed by law on all healthy political agitation, answers that it is the result of a timid unfinished reform. The rural *Junker* growls that it is nothing less than a revolution in the original principles of Prussian society. Both in a certain sense are right. The Radical could justly say the changes are neither sweeping nor secure enough to be called revolutionary; while the Conservative could reply that the uprising of 1848 frightened the king into constitutionalism, and that many leaders in that uprising now enjoy the honors and the rights of deputies. This last fact is certainly one of the most striking triumphs of an irresistible progress. That the insurrection of 1848 was a failure, in a practical sense, is beyond dispute; that it was not even politically justifiable may be pretended; but that the leaders, who afterwards became exiles, were conspirators or dangerous citizens, or anything but spirited and generous patriots, the most servile courtier will no longer assert. The vengeance of frightened princes drove them into banishment, but could not break the ties of their patriotism. When the amnesty was proclaimed after the establishment of the North German Confederation, many of the exiles returned, and, in 1870, still more came and re-entered, at once, into the political life of the fatherland. They are mostly men of education and talent; and their experience in England and America, under the operation of free institutions, does not impair their value as citizens at this stage in German history.

Dr. Loewe is a typical man of this class. The record of his life reads like a chapter out of the revolutionary history of Germany, or rather like that history itself. He was a revolutionist, but of the tribune, not of the barricades. He struggled for constitutional government in Prussia, but he preferred a peaceful, orderly struggle to foolish street conflicts which were sure to fail, and strengthened the logic as much as they hardened the heart of reaction; he was an ardent worker for German unity, and he thought it might be conquered without the aid of the cannon and the musket. But the practical moderation, the orderly and peaceful character of his method gave no security against the vengeance of governments that were resolved to repress every manifestation of liberalism. His offense was only this: after the several German governments had dissolved the Frankfort Parliament and called home the representatives, a large portion of that assembly—the Radical and advanced Liberals—adjourned in a body to Stuttgart, in Würtemberg, and organized as the "German Parliament." But here again the patriots were interrupted. The military entered the hall, and turned them out. Retaining their unity of action even in this extremity, and as if to protest by their order and moderation against the persecution of which they were the object, the little band formed upon the street, and led by Dr. Loewe, the president, and the poet Uhland, bareheaded, marched solemnly through the old Schwabian city.

For his share in this drama, Dr. Loewe was prosecuted by the Prussian government. There was some difficulty in finding a court that would make out a case. After the local court at Kalbe, the town that he represented and after which he is still called Loewe-Kalbe, had refused to entertain the case, and the criminal court at Magdeburg, entertaining it, had acquitted him, the superior court came to the rescue of reaction and found him guilty. He was sentenced to imprisonment for life, but as he had already escaped to Switzerland, the sentence amounted only to a degree of exile.

Dr. Loewe lived two years in Switzerland, two in London, and eight in New York. The latter became his second home, and, if wiser counsels had not prevailed in Germany he would doubtless have ended his days in America, in the quiet practice of his profession. Although he enjoyed high respect among his fellow exiles and emigrants in America, I believe that he never figured there in political life. This was doubtless his preference ; for no one who knows the man can doubt that his talents, if displayed, would have won as prompt and hearty recognition in the land of his adoption, as in the land of his birth.

As it is, he brought back with him, unlike some of his comrades, a just and generous affection for the country and the people that gave him an asylum. His sympathy with America, too, is not of that sentimental and fanciful sort so common in young radicals. It is the appreciation of an observer who has studied all sides of American life, and has reached a temperate, intelligent, and reasonable view. On every public and private occasion he has warmly defended the transatlantic republic. I remember one case in particular—the assassination of Lincoln. When the news of that terrible crime reached Germany, Dr. Loewe, who had known the martyr President, was the first to call the attention of the Prussian Parliament to the affair. His speech, on that occasion, was such a feeling and graceful effort, that I reproduce it in full from the translation of the American Legation. Dr. Loewe said :—

"GENTLEMEN : I have ventured to request the President to permit me to make a communication for which I claim your sympathy. That which I wish to request of you does not, indeed, belong to the immediate field of our labors, but it goes so far beyond the narrow circle of private life that, in union with a number of our colleagues, I have ventured to call your attention to it. A considerable number of our colleagues feel the need, under the dismay produced by the news of the unhappy death of President Lincoln, to give expression to their views in regard to his fate, and their sympathy with the nation from which he has been snatched away. Abraham Lincoln has fallen by the hand of an assassin, in the moment of triumph of the cause which he had conducted, and while he was in hopes of giving to his people the peace so long desired.

"Our colleagues wish, in an address, to express the sympathy not of this House,—that I say in order to remove all apprehension of a violation of the rules,—but the sympathy of the individual members of the House, in this great and unhappy event. This address we desire to present to the Minister of the United States.

"Gentlemen, I will lay the paper on the table, and I beg those of my colleagues, who share with me the feeling of warm and heartfelt sympathy in the lot of a nation which is united by so many bonds with our own people, to give expression to those feelings by appending their signatures to the address. These sympathies I regard as all the more justified, since the United States have won a new and splendid triumph for mankind, through the great struggle which they have been carrying on for the cause of true humanity, and which, as I confidently hope, in spite of this murder of their chief, they will conduct to a successful termination. In expressing our feelings of pain, we desire, at the same time, to prove our hearty sympathy with the American Nation, and those of our brothers who have taken part in the struggle for their cause. The man, gentlemen, who has fallen by the murderer's hand, and whom I seem to see with his simple, honest countenance; the man who accomplished such great deeds from the simple desire conscientiously to perform his duty; the man who never wished to be more or less than the sincere and faithful servant of his people; this man will find his own glorious place in the pages of history. . In the deepest reverence, I bow my head before this modest greatness, and I think it is especially agreeable to the spirit of my own nation, with its deep inner life and admiration of self-sacrificing devotion and effort after the ideal, to pay the tribute of veneration to such greatness, exalted as it is by its simplicity and modesty. I beg of you, gentlemen, accordingly, to join in this expression of veneration for the great dead, which, without distinction of party, we offer to him as a true servant of his State, and of the cause of humanity."

The American Minister, Mr. Judd, reporting these proceedings to the State Department, adds that "nearly the whole House rose in token of concurrence; and the address, as drawn up by the speaker, is receiving numerous signatures." It was presented on the first day of May by a committee, which was headed by Dr. Loewe, and contained furthermore Professor Virchow and Dr. Johann Jacoby, of whom the political careers are sketched in this volume, as well as Waldeck, Duncker, and some twenty others. After the proceedings, some time was spent in conversation, and Mr. Judd adds that he "parted with them (the committee) deeply gratified and consoled by this mark of generous and noble sympathy with our people and our cause." This touching demonstration, which was suggested and directed by Dr. Loewe, is only one of the many ways in which he has shown his affection for the American people.

As a speaker, Dr. Loewe is clear, positive, and forcible. A man universally respected himself, he always shows respect for his opponents; he avoids personal attacks upon others and escapes them for himself. He does not speak often now, but, perhaps, exercises the more influence.

As has been explained, he is, or long was, leader of the so-called "*Fortschritts*" party, or "Progressists," and he still holds firmly to abstract principles of advanced Liberalism. But he is a statesman and a patriot, as well as a Radical, and revolts as often from the tyranny of impracticable theories, as from that of reaction. Thus, when the late bill on military reorganization was before the *Reichstag*, he cut loose from his political friends and voted with the government. Since then, he has not formally belonged to the "Progressive" group above named, but has held an independent and somewhat isolated position.

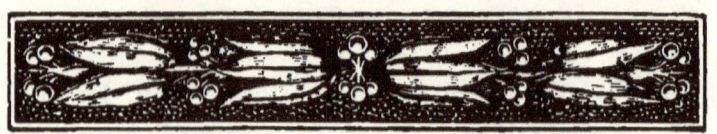

XII.

HERR SCHULZE-DELITZSCH.

THIS gentleman is a radical reformer who looks like a dull rural Conservative, a fearless and original writer, who, on the street or in his seat in Parliament, would be taken for a German Monsieur Prudhomme, the genius of sublime platitudes. Only one leading feature in his character is suggested in his face—his benevolence. His large, luminous eyes, his full, gray beard, and the slight smile about his lips seem, indeed, to exclude the restless agitator, but they reveal the generous philanthropist, the lover of the poor and the weak, the man whose heart, at least, is in the right place.

In a more rigid classification of German characters, Schulze-Delitzsch would not be ranked among the purely political leaders. He is, indeed, a politician of eminence and ability. His practical legislative triumphs outnumber, perhaps, those of some other men whose right to a place in this volume is beyond question. But Schulze's achievements as an extra-political agitator and reformer are so much more widely known, are so much more characteristic of the man, and, in fact, are the source of so much greater social benefits, that at first his introduction as a political leader seems like a displacement. This fact makes it necessary, at least, to combine with the description of the deputy some account of the social reformer. The one character almost presupposes or conditions the other; and no violence will be done to the plan of this volume, if this relation be briefly explained.

First, in a few words, the general outline of his public career; He was born on the 29th of August, 1808, in Delitzsch, in the Prussian province of Saxony, and pursued his academic and legal studies at Leipsic and Halle. On quitting the university he entered the judicial service, like so many of his colleagues, and began the ascent of the weary ladder of promotion. He was first *Referendar*, and then *Oberlandgerichts-Assessor*, in Naumburg, and finally *Kammergerichts-Assessor* in Berlin. This position he relinquished in 1841, to accept in his native city, Delitzsch, a patrimonial judgeship or judicial "living," conferred upon him by the lord of the province. This city elected him, in 1848, to the National Assembly at Berlin. In 1849, he was a member of the second Chamber, and was one of the forty-two members who, having refused, on constitutional grounds, the payment of taxes, were arraigned before the criminal court and acquitted by the jury. The speech made in self-defense by Schulze was published throughout the whole country, and made a great sensation.

On the abolition of the patrimonial courts he re-entered the service of the State, and became county judge in

Wreschen, a province of Posen; but, after a short term of service, retired definitively from the judiciary and resumed his residence at Delitzsch. From this time he devoted himself almost exclusively to the cause of the working class, for the elevation of which he had already done so much. The success which he had in organizing workingmen's associations, as well as union stores, banks, etc., is known; it provoked attention abroad, in France, Italy, Belgium, and especially England, where, by authority of the government, a series of researches into the condition of workingmen and trades-unions in Germany was made, by the well-known diplomat Monier, and his reports were published in the Blue Book. In 1859, at Weimar, was organized, under Schulze's lead, the League of German Associations, of which he was elected solicitor, and the organ of which, *Die Innung der Zukunft*, he still publishes. His ideas were further elucidated chiefly in three works,— "The Association Book," "The Loan of Credit Unions as People's Banks," and "The Laboring Classes and the Question of Association." Besides these, there appeared from his pen "Basis of a Catechism for German Workingmen," a collection of lectures that he delivered in the winter of 1862-63, before the Berlin Workingmen's Union. A little later he published a history and review of German legislation upon "Trade Unionisms." In February, 1859, under his lead, was founded, at Frankfort on the Main, the National Union, and since that time, he has devoted himself, as one of the leaders of the party of Progress, more to the political side of public life. In 1861, he was re-elected deputy, and regularly thereafter till 1873. In the *Reichstag*, from 1867 to 1874, Schulze represented the

6th district of Berlin, and now sits for the 2d district of Wiesbaden.

The above is the outline of Schulze's career, as given in the copious and discursive style of the parliamentary almanac. It wants, obviously, many details, for which the student will inquire. For instance, the explanation of Schulze's retirement from his petty judgeship in Posen is ludicrously inadequate. The almanac says he resigned because the government refused him leave of absence to visit his old home, Delitzsch. There is no hint of political difficulties. On the contrary, the offended judge is treated like an angry school-boy who leaves school, because the master will not give him a holiday. The fact is, however, that Schulze retired, like so many other liberal officials at that epoch, because his politics were offensive to the powers above him. These could not indeed openly dismiss him. Having in an unwary moment admitted him to the service because he was a promising jurist and without asking about his politics, they found him protected in his position by certain rules of the service which even they did not dare openly to violate. He could not indeed be dismissed, but he could be harassed by a petty persecution, and thus made to surrender an intolerable office. And this is what actually occurred. In the first place he early learned that promotion was not to be expected. And then such obstacles were thrown in the path of his political career, though the constitution did not exclude a judge from elective honors, that the abandonment of his judgeship became a practical condition of his success in parliamentary life. Accordingly he resigned. He returned to Delitzsch ; and since that time, he has pursued without interruption the labors of a legislator, a reformer, and a philanthropist.

In the early period of his reform labors, Schulze was greatly embarrassed for means. He himself was without fortune, and though his mother supplied from her purse the cost of lecturing tours which he undertook, she was not able to give him permanent assistance. Still he persevered nobly till 1863, when he saw the necessity of suspending his beneficent work. The Burgomastership of Delitzsch had been offered to him by the citizens, and as it assured him a fair annuity he was prepared to accept it. Then the working men came to the relief of their benefactor. A subscription for his benefit was started throughout the country. Some few men of means contributed to it, but the greatest part came from the small but numerous offerings of the poorest laboring classes. At length, the purse reached the sum of fifty thousand thalers, and it was placed at Schulze's disposition. Of course the burgomastership of Delitzsch passed into other hands. Schulze was saved for higher work. He refused to accept the fifty thousand thalers as a final gift to him. He simply accepted it in trust, bought a house at Potsdam with a portion, and invested the rest, so that only the interest accrues to his benefit. The principal belongs to the generous subscribers. The leisure and the means there acquired he devoted to his chosen mission, which he was thereby enabled to pursue on a larger scale and with greater success.

Schulze is a liberal, even a radical, and he is a reformer, but he is no revolutionist. The practical character of his method, and his objects, distinguishes him from Lasalle.

The latter was a fiery volcanic nature, and his nature gave tone to his schemes. His schemes required the aid of the state; Schulze's, only that of the working classes themselves. His method was political and revolutionary; Schulze's was economical and reformatory. Lassalle tried to array the proletariat as a fourth estate against society, against the right of property, and the obligations of religion. Schulze only organized the poor for resistance to their own worst faults. Lassalle was a brilliant orator, and a fearless agitator, and it was quite in the fitness of things that his restless life should end in a quarrel and a duel. Schulze lives to witness the success of his intelligent labors, and to enjoy the respect of all his countrymen.

The first practical realization of Schulze's plans was in the so-called *Credit und Vorschuss Vereine*, which were at once a species of savings bank, and institutions for mutual aid. The members contributed of their savings to this fund, and in their turn were aided in case of old age, sickness, or any misfortune which interrupted their daily work. The "Unions" were entirely under the management of the members. They undertook the investment of the capital, the surplus being divided annually, and they conducted the so-called "sick funds," and "funeral funds." The first one of these institutions was founded in 1850; in 1869, the number reached 1,750, of which 1,735 were in complete working order and furnished reports. These consisted of 304,000 members, and counted in their total contributions at 181,000,000 thalers. The permanent capital was 12,000,000. These concerns enjoy an admirable credit, and bankers were always ready for negotiations with them. In 1874, however, under Schulze's inspiration, a bank was founded at Berlin, like the Unions, under the control of the workingmen, and was authorized to conduct their financial transactions.

But this is not all. The indefatigable philanthropist not only organized these admirable relief societies, where the working people could have the benefit of a common fund, in case of disaster, but he also instituted co-operative or union stores, where they could purchase their household goods, and in many cases the raw material of their trades, at cost prices. These, too, were thoroughly successful, and multiplied at an unexpected rate. Whereas, in 1869, there were but 6,728 of them, to-day hardly a town or village exists without one. Their transactions per annum are reckoned by hundreds of millions, and their profits are very large. Finally, in some of the larger towns, he organized markets, where the members of the associations meet and publicly sell their wares.

Thus Schulze's efforts for the working people were of the most practical nature. He had indeed an ideal, but it was a general one ; and he tried to realize it, not by making war on all the institutions, traditions and prejudices of society, but by a patient course of education and discipline. The way to emancipate the fourth estate, in his view, was to put into its hands the elements of social strength—means, organization, unity of plan, and method. He did not ignore politics, but he reversed the method of Lassalle. The latter taught the workingmen to employ politics as a means to social position and influence. The former taught them, first, the elements of social, as the condition of political strength. Without pronouncing upon the abstract justice of their two theories, one must see and admit that the latter alone, in a military, aristocratic state, like Prussia, was likely to succeed.

Schulze is personally, however, a man of very pronounced political views. He is a member of the "Progressive" party and sits near Dr. Loewe; and represents, perhaps, the most advanced form of Liberalism recognized and tolerated by law. The next faction to the Left, the Social-democrats, are condemned by the spirit, and often by the letter, of German penal codes. He is not very prominent in debate. A new generation of men who were in their cradles when he was teaching millions of workingmen the secret of success in life, have grasped the reins of legislative power and changed the aspect of current politics.

On certain questions, however, Schulze speaks with authority and is heard with respect. One of these is the so-called "Diet question," or, paid against unpaid legislators. The delegates to the Prussian *Landtag* are regularly paid; those to the Imperial Parliament are not. This latter provision was made at the express suggestion of Prince Bismarck, and against the judgment of the great body of the Liberals. The Prince argues that the remuneration of members would fill the chamber with penniless adventurers; the Liberals claim that the opposite system gives too great advantage to rich country Conservatives. Schulze is the leading champion of this latter view. According to him the laborer is worthy of his hire. As he taught the duty of the workingman to save that which he receives, so he teaches the right of the legislator to receive that which he earns. Schulze's demonstration on this subject is one of the annual parliamentary events. Each session he brings in his familiar resolution instructing the government to submit a bill for paying the members of the *Reichstag;* it is regularly passed by a large majority ; and it is regularly laid aside without action by the government. It is, of course, hardly necessary to mention that Schulze is watchful of legislation affecting the interest of his chosen clients ; and as much by the respect felt for his unselfish advocacy, as by the soundness and moderation of his views, he carries great weight with his colleagues.

In the early part of this sketch it is said that the appearance of Schulze, as he sits quietly in his place in Parliament, suggests the worthy Jacques Prudhomme, the genius of common-place. But appearances deceive. Instead of being a mere empiric, a shoemaker or a blacksmith out of place, he is really a scholar and a thinker. Because he does not give the workingmen incendiary ideas, it would be false to conclude that he gives them no ideas. On the contrary, Schulze tries to improve not only the bodies, but also the minds of his clients ; not only their actual position in society, but also the reasoning which they apply to the solution of social problems. The pamphlets that he has published, the lectures that he gives to the workingmen, the speeches that he makes in Parliament, are the work of a philosopher rather than of a demagogue.

I have included Schulze-Delitzsch among the political leaders of Germany, not so much because of any great prominence that he has, as a parliamentarian, as because of the influence that he exerts among the working classes. Having called them into being as a political force, he has a right to direct them. Having this force at his disposal, he has won the respect of society by the moderate and just use that he has made of it.

Since the above was written, the annual reports, of the various Associations for the fiscal year, 1874, have been published. They make a substantial volume, which contains not only the reports and statistics of the separate societies, of course in a condensed form, but also a general report from the solicitor himself. As it may be of interest to compare the figures above given with those for the year 1874, I transcribe, from an analysis in the *Deutsche Rundschau*, the leading points in the last report. From this the reader will gain a renewed appreciation of Schulze's beneficent labors. These reports certainly do not appear so promptly as most of the commercial reports, but for a sufficient reason, because the editor must collate the annual balances of many hundred associations. If one only considers this, one will be astonished at the rapidity of this important mathematical work. It requires the entire attention of a man like Schulze-Delitzsch, and the strong support which he finds in his first secretary, Dr. F. Schneider. The generally encouraging growth of the Association has been uninterruptedly maintained in 1874. In what concerns the most important matter, that of the Relief Unions and People's Banks, it appears that 2409 have grown to 2639. The 815 which sent reports for 1874 to the General Agency at Potsdam, counted on an average 504 members, an increase of 25 since 1873; and they have 1335 3-4 millions of marks on deposit. Since, however, the loans on valuables and the current credits show a decrease as compared with 1873, while only the credits on exchange and mortgages have increased, it would seem that the injurious effects of the financial crisis made themselves felt less keenly among the poorer artisans, than among the rich. There is, in the judgment of the solicitor, renewed cause for warning the Association against the misuse of the funds by regular patrons; against the investment of funds in mortgages, and against imprudent meddling with securities. In membership, the mechanics, as before, outnumber any other class, but they have fallen to something more than a third of the whole. The farmers make something more than a fifth, the tradesmen a tenth, the hired laborers a little less than a tenth; these latter are on the increase. If we examine the Associations according to the separate occupations, they seem to grow, above all, among farmers. Instead of 150, there are this time 189 among this class. Their aim is in part, the procuring in common, seed, implements, etc., in part, the sale in common, of milk, butter, cheese, hops, wine, and other products. The increase of the specially interesting "Productive Associations"—shops and manufactories in possession of the laborers, *i. e.* where the laborer is also partner—was not affected by the disorders in trade in 1874. From 162 in the year 1873, the number has increased to 202, which is 20 per cent. As to the affairs of these enterprises, it must be admitted, as was foreseen in 1874, that they have not been altogether favorable. Instead of 30, only 20 have sent their yearly statements. That the number is relatively small, is explained by the nature of the Association. The "Consumption Unions," in number 42 more than in 1873, still sell too much on credit. With the "Building Unions," the efforts of the leading members ought to be toward the choice of houses for single families, since the tendency in great cities is toward an excess of vast barracks, that are so bad for the moral and physical conditions of the occupants. In view of the general derangement and partial prostration of business in the year 1874, the progress and condition of these excellent institutions must be regarded as favorable and satisfactory.

XIII.

JOHANN JACOBY.

D<small>R.</small> JACOBY is no longer, strictly, a representative leader of the present race of politicians. With the war of 1870, his public life practically closed, and his seat, which he still retains in the Lower Prussian House, is rather a tribute to his past achievements than to his actual influence. But he is an indispensable link between the new era and the old. He is a representative of that grave and stormy period militant, without a knowledge of which the present era cannot be understood and ought not to be studied. He has endured persecution and has suffered injustice; he has held his head erect in the presence of kings; and he has never failed to be the fearless and eloquent champion of popular rights. A practical physician, like Dr. Loewe, he is also an example of what may be called the purely political, in distinction from the semi-social or semi-judicial reformer. I have already described Lasker as a politician who never quite forgets the lawyer, and Schulze as one who uses political means chiefly to further extra-political reforms. Dr. Loewe, on the contrary, is a politician only for the sake of politics, and the same is true of Jacoby.

Johann Jacoby was born in the city of Königsberg, on the 1st of May, 1805, of Jewish parents. He studied from 1823 to 1827, at the University of Königsberg; took his diploma as doctor of medicine at Berlin, and, in 1830, after extensive travel, settled in his native city and began the practice of his profession. About the same time, he began the practice of politics.

Up to the year 1840, he was active in local affairs, wrote frequently for Radical papers, and often came into conflict with the censorship. The people had abandoned all hope of a constitution from Frederic William III. The memory of his broken pledges, of course, remained, and it was known that he had never failed to impress upon his son and heir apparent, the folly of believing in "abstract theories;" but his old age and his personal amiability softened the opposition to the later years of his reign. In Königsberg, which, as the king's residence while an exile during the French occupation, was associated with some of his bitterest trials, he enjoyed more than ordinary esteem. The "Estates" of the oldest province in the Prussian monarchy, had not yet received the royal rebuke which called forth so indignant a protest from Jacoby.

Frederic William III. died in 1840, and his son Frederic William IV. ascended the throne. Instantly, the whole face of politics was changed. That wide spread feeling of discontent, that resolute spirit of reform, which had been so patientand forbearing under the old régime, now awoke armed against the new king from the start. Among the first and the boldest to act was Dr. Jacoby.

The king, following the practice of his family, went to Königsberg to receive the homage of his faithful East Prussian subjects. He was gracious and benevolent. From many sides, and it is even said from the king himself, the wish was expressed that the Provincial Estates should lay before him the questions that concerned them. The Estates of East Prussia did this frankly and fearlessly. In answer to an inquiry of the king, which of their privileges they would like to see specially confirmed, they replied that "it was not their 'privileges' about which they had to address their king, but a right of the nation, which had its roots in the Law of May 22d, 1815, and the fulfilment of which they demanded." His Majesty politely, but firmly, declined to accept such a theory. The example of East Prussia was followed by other provinces, and the answer in each case was the same, though the tone became less and less gracious. In 1841, the demands of the province of Silesia were rejected almost ungraciously.

At this crisis, a pamphlet appeared in Strasburg and was circulated over Germany. It was called "Four Questions answered by an East Prussian."* "Like a thunder-clap," says Dr. Guido Weiss, "it fell upon Prussia, upon all Germany. I, who first learned from this work to think politically, received in South Germany immediately the impression, which, perhaps, beyond the author's expectation, it there made. How the Frenchified rhetorical Liberalism of a Rotteck or a Welcker disappeared before the granite strength, before the iron logic, in the works of the Northerner! At that time, the opinion was firmly rooted

---

* "*Vier Fragen beantwortet von einem Ostpreussen.*"

that the history of constitutionalism in Prussia would be the history of the constitution for Germany. Johann Jacoby was the author. Who was the man? It was learned that he was a Königsberg physician, highly esteemed at home for his pure, solid character, and for the professional fidelity which he had always shown, and, especially, during a season of cholera; that he was a friend of the Minister von Schön."*

This "epoch-making" work proposed the four questions:—"What do the Estates wish?"—"What justifies them?"—"What decision was given them?"—"What remains for them to do?" To the last of these it answers: "That which they have hitherto as a favor requested, now, as a proved right, to demand."

Modesty, not fear, led Jacoby to publish his pamphlet anonymously, for he mailed a copy directly to the king, and wrote on the title page, with an audacity to which his majesty was not accustomed: "I am the author, Johann Jacoby, Doctor of Medicine, Königsberg." The king promptly gave an order for his arrest and examination. He was accused of nothing less than high treason. Being called upon to name his accomplices, he replied that only the history of his country and the ministers, Stein and Hardenberg, in their writings and reform measures, shared his guilt. By the Superior Court of Berlin, before which he was tried, he was found guilty, and sentenced to two years imprisonment, and loss of honor. Jacoby appealed to the *Obertribunal*, and was unconditionally acquitted, but

---

* Dr. Guido Weiss—Speech in the Second Election District of Berlin.

the protocol of the deliberations, the grounds of the verdict, were refused him. It is considered significant that the veteran president of this court, Grollmann, was soon afterwards retired by the government.

Of Jacoby's character, as developed at this time, Dr. A. Jung writes as follows: "Jacoby is a man of iron logic, a man of Catonian tirelessness. He has two practical instruments, with which he demonstrates and refutes, with which he accuses and defends: these are the existing law, and an intense brevity of style. The graceful form, the bold forehead, the intelligent, mild, blue eye, the beardless, open countenance of Jacoby, invite confidence. He does not ask frivolous questions; he does not make frivolous remarks; he is too deeply engrossed in himself and a definite object; he is a man of the strictest reserve and precision; a foe of speaking for the sake of speaking; scarcely a friend of reflection, rather only of events, of facts, of the historical moment, of the concrete present. Thus, he is an enemy of extravagance and of inadequacy of expression, an admirer of the simple, unpretending, even to the matter of dress, yet this latter must be proper for his appearance, at any time, to defend the rights of the people. We recognize, thankfully, in him great services, a brilliant understanding; we must give full credit to his comprehensive scientific culture. Jacoby is, in a high sense, a respected character in our city, a man of unusual studies. By profession a physician, he is one of those firmly and clearly marked individualities, whose unbending consistency and tendency to refer everything to an existing law, seem to have predestined them, at once, to medicine, jurisprudence, and politics; in short, an individuality whose whole career expresses that ethical coldness, that predominance of indifference, that unshaken calmness, which Spinoza laid down as inherent in the Jewish nature, and in his own life so strikingly exemplified." *

Scarcely was Jacoby out of the dangers provoked by his "Four Questions," than he took up his pen again, and sent out, one after another, a series of bold, trenchant, and effective pamphlets. In 1844, he published, "On the Right of an Acquitted Person to demand a Statement of the Reasons of the Judgment." Next, in the same year, appeared "The Ro.al Word of Frederic William III. "Finally, "Prussia in the Year 1845." ** These publications drew down another accusation, and he was again acquitted.

With the year 1848, Jacoby's parliamentary career began. Almost at the same time, he was elected to the Lower House of the Prussian "National Assembly" and to the German Parliament at Frankfort on the Main. In the latter he was the successor of Frederic von Raumer, the great historian, and friend of America. When Prussia re-called her delegates, Jacoby was naturally one of those who disputed the right of the government thus to command the representatives of the people, and he was one of the faithful little band who followed Dr. Loewe to Stuttgart. After the dissolution of this assembly, Jacoby, like the other leaders, fled to Switzerland, and, like them, was prosecuted for treason. He did not, however, like them, accept a trial and conviction

---

* Dr. A. Jung—*Königsberg und die Königsberger.*

* * The German titles are respectively:

"*Ueber das Recht des Freigesprochenen die Ausfertigung des wider ihn ergangenen Erkenntnisses zu verlangen,*" "*Das Königliche Wort Friedrich Wilhelms III.,*" and "*Preussen im Jahre* 1845."

in contumaciam. He was not willing, from a safe asylum, to laugh at the impotence of his persecutors. With a boldness which has few examples, and which the prudent patriot who might not approve, was forced to admire, he obeyed the summons of the court, returned to Königsberg, and took his place in the prisoner's box. The penalties of treason in those days were not light. According to the ancient law, then in force, the crime of high treason could be punished by dragging the victim to the place of execution, breaking his body upon a wheel, and exposing the fragments in public.

Jacoby himself made a speech for the defence, in the course of which he gave an eloquent statement of his political theories and aims. "I belong to the extreme opposition," he said, "but against injustice and untruth. I only did what I held to be my duty; I remained at the post which my constituents entrusted to me. Three times have I been arraigned for political offences, three times have the courts of the country acquitted me. In those cases I had maintained, as a publicist, the right of the people of Prussia to a representative constitution, and the very next years justified my demand; in the present case I have maintained, as a member of Parliament, the right of the German people to a free and united country. Hopeless as the present appears, the day will yet come, when the justice of this demand will be admitted. The judgment here belongs to no earthly court; here history alone has the decision. Here lies before you, gentlemen of the jury, an unspotted and blameless record." The trial lasted nine hours, the deliberations of the jury one hour, and the verdict was an acquittal. The result was a great surprise to the party of reaction. So sure were the authorities of conviction that the wagon which was to convey the accused to prison, was drawn up before the door of the court house; and to quell the expected popular tumult the streets were lined with grenadiers. The verdict was received with great enthusiasm, in which even the soldiers, who had been introduced into the room for a different purpose, could not be kept from sharing.

In the order of time, however, this remarkable incident in Jacoby's life is preceded by one quite as remarkable and even more dramatic. I have said above that he was a member of the First Prussian Assembly. It was a stormy and critical season. On the 1st of November, a semi-liberal ministry, at the head of which stood Herr von Pfuel, had been replaced by a reactionary ministry, under Count von Brandenburg. On the 2d, this new cabinet appeared before the assembly. With the first words that were exchanged, the hopes of reconciliation and harmony fell, and the excitement which reigned throughout the whole country, found expression in the chamber. It was resolved to send on the same day a deputation to the king at Potsdam to declare to him that co-operation with such a ministry was impossible, and to represent to him the danger of continuing in the course just adopted. The deputies were received by the king in the old castle of Sans Souci. It is full of the relics, and sacred to the memory of Frederic the Great; and it is possible that Frederic William IV. hoped to acquire in this historical place some of the spirit of his great ancestor for the coming trial. The deputation was ushered in by an adjutant; Jacoby was of the number. An address was handed to the king, who accepted it in silence, and turned to leave. Jacoby stepped forward: "We are not come," said he, "simply to present this address, but also to render Your Majesty a report on the state of the country. Will you listen to us?" "No!" said the king, and turned his back upon the deputies. Then Jacoby drew back, and said to his comrades, but with resolute and emphatic tones, which rang through the palace: "That is the misfortune of kings, that they are not willing to hear the truth!"

It appears that this was considered an astounding breach of etiquette, but nothing more serious. The courts did not take it up. A school of timid Liberals pretended that Jacoby's bold words had really done harm to the cause of reform by incensing the king, and making future concessions more difficult; and the immediate events did seem to confirm the view.

The king honored the address with a written answer, which was read the next day in the Assembly. It was what courtiers call a "Royal answer." His majesty said that Count Brandenburg possessed his confidence; that he represented principles which were his own and should never be sacrificed; and that he saw no reason for dismissing the new ministry. Two or three days later, the minister-president appeared to the House and read a "royal message," adjourning the *Landtag* to the city of Brandenburg, in order "to secure it from seditious outbreaks in the capital." The House murmured, and the minister, declared that a royal order was not debatable. Nevertheless the House did debate it, and boldly resolved that, as it saw no ground for transferring its sittings to Brandenburg, it would remain in Berlin. Some of the deputies proved timid and hesitating; Jacoby was one of those who did not flinch. The sessions were held in the royal theatre, and were guarded by the "Citizens' Guard," a species of municipal militia. On the morning of the 10th of November, it was known that the government was resolved to introduce the troops of the line, to disperse the assembly, and to close the doors of the theatre. About noon, the soldiers appeared, Field-marshal Wrangel at their head; a parley followed with the Citizens' Guard; a conflict, violence, and bloodshed seemed inevitable, when the deputies, yielding to overpowering force, left the hall in a body, and abandoned the field to the soldiery. Adolph Stahr gives a graphic account of this closing scene : "The President of the National Assembly arose, and said : 'The force must be recognized. In the name of the National Assembly, which yields before it, I protest most solemnly against this act of military violence. The session is adjourned until to-morrow morning.' The target clubs formed *espaliers*. As the president, at the head of the Assembly, issued from the House, the Citizens' Guard presented arms. The president took the arm of the commander of the guard, and the deputies left the House in pairs, arm-in-arm, and silent, followed by the people, whose sympathetic cheers and hurras rang out far into the night. The battalions of Citizens' Guard closed up the column, marching with their hats on their bayonets. The 'Commanding General in the Mark,' was alone with his troops, on the broad square."*

Jacoby's initiation into parliamentary life was therefore a stormy one, and he did not reach calmer times for many

---

* A. Stahr—*Die Preussische Revolution*, Vol. II, p. 368.

years. Turned out of doors with the Prussian Assembly, by force of bayonets, he shared six months later in the unhappy fate of the Rump Parliament, at Stuttgart. This has already been described. In Prussia, after the events above related, the constitutional question was long in suspense, until the king, finally, declining the aid or counsels of the people's representatives, ordered his jurists to draft a charter, and proclaimed it as an act of royal grace. From that time, the reaction had full power. The Democratic party, and with it Jacoby, retired practically from public affairs. From 1850 to 1863, Jacoby quietly practised his profession at Königsberg.

On the change of dynasty, in 1861, the Radicals emerged again from their retirement. At the first election after the convention, a popular rebuke was administered to the reactionary and arrogant language of the new king by the return of an unusually large opposition majority, which included nearly all the leading Radicals. Waldeck, the worthy leader of the Prussian democracy, Dr. Loewe, and many others who had long been in retirement or exile, were in the new House. Only Jacoby was absent. "Acting shrewdly," says Wolfgang Menzel,* "he had refused an election, because his time was not yet come." Two years later, it seems, he recognized the propitious hour. Herr von Bismarck had just accepted the premiership; and as he was known to be a resolute man as well as a strict Conservative, the conditions of a serious conflict were easily perceived. To remain silent and inactive in such a crisis was cowardice. Jacoby accepted a candidature in a district of Königsberg, was elected, and took his seat in the Lower House.

---

* Wolfgang Menzel—*Der Deutsche Krieg*, Vol. I, p. 100.

The eulogists whom I have above quoted, agree in calling Jacoby a man of "iron consistency." He was to have occasion to vindicate his consistency in a striking way, against temptations to which the lofty Christian virtue of his colleagues ignominiously surrendered. It was, of course, natural that he should oppose, with all the Liberals and Radicals, the unconstitutional means by which the Danish war was organized, as well as the unholy alliance by which it was fought and won. But, while they denounced as illegal the taxes levied in contempt of Parliament, the Liberal deputies were not ashamed to accept their fees out of the proceeds of such levies. Not so Jacoby. He, and he alone of all the deputies, declared that he would not, by accepting his deputy's pay at the hands of the government, give even a constructive recognition of the spoliated treasure of the State ; and poor as he was, and depending almost on his pay for his support, he steadfastly refused to compromise with his principles. As the war with Austria drew near, he labored hard to organize public opinion against it. At his suggestion, the different election districts of Berlin adopted a protest, which declared that the war was "unjustifiable and immoral." Prussia "had no right to the Duchies, and they alone and Parliament had the authority to decide on their fate."

Finally, after Sadowa, Jacoby did not stultify himself, in an excess of unreflecting patriotism. He stubbornly refused to condone an unjust war, or a war which he held to be unjust, because the aggressor had been crowned by victory. The so-called "vote of indemnity" did not receive his support. His appearance in the debate is thus described by his enemy Menzel : "In the debate upon the address to the throne, the old Königsberg Jew Jacoby could not refrain from obtruding his intolerable harangues. In his speech, the Jew recognized magnanimously the bravery of the Prussian army, but said the war was undertaken without, even against, the will of the people, and the victory would profit not the popular party, but only the supreme commander of the armies. In spite of this victory, the war had brought neither honor to the Prussian people, nor healing to the German fatherland. The present never judged itself impartially. The future would show whether the day of Biarritz was more fortunate than that of Olmütz. The people wished a united, the war had only brought a divided Germany. To strengthen Prussia was not to strengthen Germany. Should the existing governmental system continue in Prussia, the new organization of Germany would be to the old, like death to sickness. The government demands indemnity; but for a prolonged, unconstitutional, irresponsible régime no assembly of the people could grant indemnity, if the old ministers kept their places." *

It is well known that these views did not prevail. Still, Jacoby had vindicated his consistency and his courage, he had shown that most elevated sort of control which, in a spirit of justice, can withstand the intoxication of a great national triumph.

Once more—and it was Jacoby's last prominent act—he tried to breast a popular current which he thought treacherous and threatening. It was during the war with France and shortly after the battle of Sedan; when that great

---

* W. Menzel—*Der Deutsche Krieg*, Vol. II. p. 118.

victory, followed as it was by the capitulation of Metz, seemed to decide the fate of France, and to render the end of the struggle only a question of time, the exultant patriots at home began to discuss the conditions of peace. Details were, of course, avoided, but upon one thing there was an emphatic harmony of opinion : Alsace and Lorraine must be annexed. Military interests and geographical interests, the rights of original possession and the ties of language, were all invoked to justify the popular claim. It seemed temerity and folly to oppose it. But the "old Königsberg Jew," who had so often braved in behalf of the people the terrors of a military despotism, was not afraid, obeying his own conscience, to brave the rash impulses of the people themselves. In a public speech made at Königsberg, Jacoby said that the forcible annexation of Alsace and Lorraine would be an act of intolerable injustice. Unless those provinces were asked, and freely sanctioned a change, it ought not to be effected. The military commander at Königsberg, having no more formidable foe before him, at once opened war upon a single man, and through him, upon the principle of freedom of speech. This time the authorities did not commit the fault of bringing the accused before a court, where he would be sure of acquittal. By order of the commander, he was arrested and shut up in a fortress.

The counsel of Jacoby, having exhausted all other means, made a direct application to Bismarck, then in camp before Paris, for the release or immediate trial of his client. The application was denied. By this time, the affair had become generally known, and made a great sensation, not only in Germany, where the press still retained some self-respect, but also in England, where it provoked comments little flattering and very embarrassing for the victorious Prussian statesman. It was in danger of neutralizing the satisfaction with which even the friends of Germany hailed her triumph in the field. Finally the reaction came. After Jacoby had been three weeks in prison, another application was made by his counsel, and Bismarck replied that his majesty had ordered his release. Arrested without any legal warrant, he was in the same way discharged, without any legal satisfaction. Although he lodged with the State prosecutor a charge of false imprisonment against the general—that was his only relief. To this day, the officer has never been punished.

The features in Jacoby's character and the incidents in his life, as they have been described in this short sketch, fully justify his choice as one of the subjects of this volume. His active career is indeed ended. But as the type of a fearless Radical, and a just patriot,—a Radical who never wavered in the cruel days of adversity, a patriot who could reason even with a delirium of national exultation,—a man whose virtue, defending the gravest political principles, would not tamper with the most transient question of ethics,—a man thus endowed by nature and formed by discipline—Jacoby deserves the study and admiration of the present, as he enjoyed the respect of the last generation. At the same time, these very traits made it impossible that Jacoby should ever become a statesman, in the ordinary sense of the term. His work was the assertion of abstract political principles, without bargains, compromises, or concessions; but this is not, in a strict sense, statesmanship. In a good, and not a bad sense, he was a revolutionist. His methods were destructive; of the bad, it is true, but still destructive, and not constructive. He stubbornly resisted evil measures, but a policy of exclusive resistance seldom reaches positive ends. As he is not a statesman with a carefully developed programme, so he is not an orator with a thoroughly trained art. His strength as a speaker lies rather in the point and pregnancy of his epigrammatic remarks, in the intense sincerity of his convictions, in the imposing boldness of his manner. No great speeches of his survive. He is a fine scholar and a clear writer; but he is too earnest a man to waste time in balancing phrases and composing antitheses.

XIV.

HERR HASSELMANN.

THE right of the Social-democrats to a representative in these pages is happily, or unhappily, beyond dispute. Their numbers in the *Reichstag*, and the powerful constituency that stands behind them, as well as their noisy and obtrusive boldness, compel even the most unwilling chronicler to give them notice. And this compliment is after all a feeble one, when compared with the splendid homage paid to them by the imperial government. If all other means of notoriety failed the socialist faction ; if there were no other reason for devoting an article to their restless agitation, both the means and the reason could be found in the exceptional honor paid them by the ministers, the legislators, the police, and the courts of the German Empire. So important was this element, even in 1871, that the new constitution expressly put it under imperial supervision, by authorizing the *Reichstag* to legislate on the subjects of the press and public meetings. The article has been loyally and abundantly enforced. Scarcely a session has passed without some bill, directly or indirectly aimed at the agitation of the Socialistic and Democratic party. Next to the army, the Workingmen's Union has been the object of greatest solicitude to the imperial chancelry. It deserves, therefore, to be described as one among the political factions and forces of Germany, and its representative has a right to rank among the political leaders.

It is true that the claim of Hasselmann to act or appear as this representative, does not command the same unconditional acquiescence. He is only one among many equals, if not among some superiors. The so-called "Social-democratic party" in the *Reichstag* numbers but nine members; but of these, three may fairly compete with Hasselmann for the leadership, and two of these even represent a rival and in some respects opposite policy. Hasenclever, the colleague and friend of Hasselmann, is the president of the "General Workingmen's Union of Germany,"* and from the position derives great authority. Bebel and Liebknecht are Saxons; their headquarters are at Leipsic, whence they issue the *Volksstaat*, and they are deeply interested in the "International," instead of the "Workingmen's Union." But these schisms and feuds will be explained in another place. Hasselmann's position and his career are both striking enough to be representative of the Socialistic agitation in Germany, and no further explanation of the choice is necessary.

It is, however, necessary to give some account of the organization of the workingmen as a political party, for,

---

* *Allgemeiner Deutscher Arbeiter-Verein.*

without it, the leaders of that party cannot be understood. In the sketch of Schulze-Delitzsch, the antagonism between that Teutonic "Poor Richard," and the more radical and sweeping schemes of Lassalle, were briefly hinted at, but were not explained at length. This antagonism, which at last became a personal quarrel, is the indispensable key to the earlier stages of the Socialistic agitation. And since Schulze, as a living leader, has already been sketched, it will only be necessary to give some account of a rival far more audacious, far more brilliant, and far less fortunate.

Ferdinand Lassalle was in all respects one of the most remarkable men whom modern Germany has produced. A Jew by descent and a friend of Heine, he had the restless energy of his race and the pitiless radicalism of his master. He was no *Sans-culotte*, no vulgar conspirator, no unlettered demagogue. He passed the gymnasium and the university, and studied law and philosophy as far as the best teachers of Germany could carry him. With working men he had no sort of class sympathy. He took up their cause merely out of the impulse of a generous heart, a burning hatred of oppression and injustice, a philosophic discontent with the real or fancied evils of existing society. If he had been an American, with the same nature, he would have been a determined Abolitionist. In Germany, he thought the working classes were the victims of a false adjustment of social relations ; and, when this conviction had once taken possession of his soul, he served it with all the loyalty of his fiery nature.

His chivalrous espousal, when only twenty years old, of the cause of the unfortunate Countess Hatzfeld, is one of the most romantic incidents of real life ; and it was made more remarkable by the fidelity and enthusiasm with which that aristocratic lady long supported the socialistic schemes of her champion. His oratory was powerful and brilliant, and a reference to it stirs the blood of all who ever sat beneath its charms. It was not musical and persuasive, but trenchant, imposing, and commanding; fearless and ready in retort, terrible in the force of invective. He once spoke three days in self-defence before a court at Cologne, and his speech is studied as a model, even by aspiring conservatives. Lassalle was a born agitator, if not revolutionist, and he made war upon society till his death. His ideal was the *Volksstaat*, the people's state, which he set up in contrast to the state of the aristocracy and the bourgeoisie, and his scheme included in its details the most comprehensive and immediate interference of the State in the interest of the proletariat.

Lassalle's violent career met a violent end, and after that, a schism broke out in the ranks of his followers. At first it was rather a geographical difference. The headquarters of Lassalle had been at Leipsic, and the Saxon Socialists, as the most active and numerous, demanded that Leipsic should continue to be the centre of agitation. Their champion, who is alone worthy to be the successor of Lassalle, is Carl Marx, who, if he were not an exile, would be the real leader of the working-men in Germany. Marx is the founder of the "International," which made a great deal of unnecessary noise. This was a step in advance of Lassalle, though it may easily be sustained on his theories. The organ of this party is the *Volksstaat*, which is published at Leipsic. The Berlin party centred around the "General Workingmen's Union of Germany," of which the president was Herr von Schweitzer. Its organ is the *Neuer Social-Democrat.*

Between the principles, if the word may be used, of those two organizations, there is no perceptible difference. Both worship the name and memory of Lassalle, and both claim to have no other aim than faithfully to further the dissemination of his ideas, and to procure the triumph of his theories. But they differ about the means to be employed. The Leipsic party believes in an international league and a simultaneous agitation of workingmen in all countries. The Berlin party, on the contrary, prefers to organize the Germans by themselves, and by concentrating their energies, to render success more speedy and certain.

Marx was an exile in England, and the control of the Leipsic party, and the representation of the International in Germany, passed into the hands of three men, Bebel, Liebknecht, and Becker. The latter is the pamphleteer of the concern, and innumerable brochures from his pen may be bought by those who have the curiosity or the time to read them. The other two are members of the *Reichstag*. It has, however, been their misfortune to spend in prison a good portion of the time which might, otherwise, have been devoted to the legislation of their country; and their reputation, as parliamentarians, is yet to be made. The only occasion on which I had the honor of hearing Herr Bebel, was in January last. The Chancellor of the Empire, Prince Bismarck, had made a long speech against the press and socialism, and had mentioned, incidentally, the sympathy of the social democrats with the commune of Paris. Bebel did not deny the fact, but he opposed the inference drawn from it. He mounted the speaker's platform, and, under cover of a personal explanation, was gesticulating wildly and declaiming like an injured patriot, when a parliamentary rule, enforced by the chairman, cut him ignominiously off. He is an impassioned, vigorous speaker, not without a certain force. Liebknecht is a more politic man, a pamphleteer like Becker, and he and Bebel are always mentioned together, like Beaumont and Fletcher.

In the meantime, the Berlin party has also passed into other hands. Schweitzer had become too conservative for the younger men. A coalition was formed against him, and he was expelled as a traitor. The two ungrateful disciples, whom he had trained and brought forward, divided the succession between them. Hasenclever became president of the Union, Hasselmann editor of the *Neuer Social-Democrat*. The former is the practical man of business, the organizer, the executive-manager. The latter is the literary apostle, the fiery advocate of the cause. They work together as harmoniously and efficiently as Bebel and Liebknecht at Leipsic, and among such turbulent and disorderly spirits, present a strange spectacle of peaceful co-operation.

Wilhelm Hasselmann was born on the 25th of September, 1844, in Bremen. He studied at the polytechnic school at Hanover, and, with a view to becoming a chemist, at the Universities of Göttingen and Berlin. This academic career, which would perhaps have made an excellent conservative physicist, he interrupted suddenly, and embraced the cause and the fortunes of the Socialist party. He seems to have preferred the elements of society to those of nature, for his experiments. His merits as a club orator attracted the notice of Schweitzer, who made him a Secretary of the Union, and afterwards an assistant editor of the *Social-Democrat.* When Schweitzer was expelled, as above stated, Hasselmann naturally succeeded him in the chief-editorship. In a business sense, the sheet is a great success, and its daily circulation is said to number over 20,000 copies. No small share of this is due to the literary contributions of Hasselmann. Day by day, for several years, he has covered the first page of that sheet with his revolutionary proclamations, in which indefinite cures for undefined evils are set forth with all the delightful candor of his class.

Judged by the standard of his readers, Hasselmann's literary capacity is, no doubt, considerable. Dr. Rudolph Meyer speaks of it in terms of praise : " The present man of science, of the Union," he says, "is Hasselmann, whom von Schweitzer engaged as sub-editor. He speaks fluently, and writes *à la Marat."* * And again Meyer says : " Since the Union owns only three sheets, it has but few writers. After the talented Dr. von Schweitzer, who was familiar with many sciences, had been expelled, the party had no representative of much learning. The editor Hasselmann has pursued no regular course of study, but was brought into the right course by Schweitzer, and has made himself well informed on Socialistic systems, and in the revolutionary history of France. What he lacks in deep knowledge, he makes up by a great literary talent. Of all

---

* *Der Emancipationskampf des vierten Standes in Deutschland.* Berlin, 1874, p. 98.

Social-democrats he has the most effective style for the workingmen." *

After this, the reader will, perhaps, be anxious to have a specimen of the German Marat's workmanship. The Socialists of Germany borrow many of their favorite words from the jargon of their brethren in France, *Bourgeoisie, proletariat, canaille*, etc., being common to both. Hasselmann, in particular, who makes a speciality of French history, and above all French revolutionary history, abounds in terms familiar to students of radical Paris literature. He loves to picture to himself a German reign of terror, like that of Paris; he imitates the style of the club orator of that age, and, in many respects, perhaps unconsciously, the same language comes to serve him and them. The following extract is from one of Hasselmann's favorite compositions, entitled *Die Canaille*, which may be called in English, "The Rabble."

"Who are the men with muscles firm as iron, but with pale and haggard faces, who hold watch by the glow of furnaces, and earn their bread in the light of molten iron? Who are the men that guide the noisy machines in the dust and racket of factories, and under whose hands the most wonderful products of skilful industry come into being? Who are the men that build the palaces in heat and cold, in sunshine and rain, under the open heavens? Who are the men that laboriously guide the plough over the fields and wrest from the soil its products?

"Ask the frivolous dandy, ask the insolent country

---

* *Der Emancipationskampf des vierten Standes in Deutschland.* Berlin, 1874, p. 150.

squire, ask the covetous usurer, ask all those who live and riot in palaces, and squander the labor of others; they will tell you.

"They will say: 'These are the rabble!' Who is yonder woman, who crouches in her wretched hovel over the corpse of her husband, whom they brought in to her, dead and mangled in the service of capital? Who are the children that, starving and freezing, must roam about in the early morning among smoking chimneys? Who are the maidens who wander homeless and in despair, a child on the breast, cast out by human society, or who have already thrown away shame, and in velvet and silk, but with empty hearts and sore bodies, hunted by the police, hurry through the streets?

"Ask the speculators in women and children, ask the seducers; they will not fail to give you an answer.

"They will say: 'This is the rabble!'

* * * * * * * * *

"Yes, 'the people is a rabble,' as long as the bourgeois society subsists. Lassalle declared once, with bitter irony, that if the liberal press received the order to print this sentence at the head of every journal, it would not dare, in its cowardice, to disobey. It is a bitter misfortune that the order is not given; for, day by day, the people must read that, so long as it does not itself put its hand to the work in order to break road for the new Social institutions, it is not, and under the pressure of the hard law of wages cannot be anything else than the suffering, despised rabble.

"People, learn to understand your misery; people, reflect that your inconstancy and sluggishness alone bear the blame, if we do not arise and force the recognition of the rights of man in the State."

This is the sort of literature on which German Socialism thrives. It is easy to recognize in it the violence of Marat, though the German *Canaille* are perhaps not expected to know, that Marat was more than a mere phrase-maker; that he did not hide an intellectual or a moral timidity under the cover of rattling words, but went straight to his meaning with a ferocious but effective frankness. Still, the leading articles of Hasselmann, as the best that are to be obtained, have upon the workingmen an influence, of which the historian is unfortunately obliged to take account.

At the last general election Hasselmann was a candidate in many districts, but suceeded in barely carrying one of them. In the district of Elberfeld-Barmen, where there are large manufactories, and a large industrious population, he succeeded in gaining the poll over his national liberal competitor by a majority of just 381, in a total vote of 25,000. But this slender margin was enough to fill the hearts of his constituents with present joy, and their souls with visions of future glory. One old woman, in her enthusiasm, burned her spinning-wheel, her only means of support; but in a neighboring district, where the Socialist candidate was defeated, a young laborer was heard to sigh, "Alas! now we must continue to eat bread and potatoes."

It is probable, nevertheless, that the legislative achievements of the deputy Hasselmann do not quite come up to the hopes of his ardent electors. The reader will recall the famous figure, which Edmund Burke in his "Reflections on the Revolution in France," used to describe certain English sympathizers with that revolution. "The vanity, restlessness, petulance, and spirit of intrigue, of several petty cabals, who attempt to hide their total want of consequence in bustle and noise, and puffing and mutual quotation of each other, make you imagine that our contemptuous neglect of their abilities is a mark of general acquiescence in their opinions. No such thing, I assure you. Because half a dozen grasshoppers, under a fern, make a field ring with their importunate chink, while thousands of great cattle repose beneath the shadow of the British oak, chew the cud and are silent, pray do not imagine that these who make the noise are the only inhabitants of the field; that, of course, they are many in number, or, that after all, they are other than the little shrivelled, meagre, hopping, though loud and troublesome insects of the hour." The application to the Social-democrats, in the *Reichstag*, is incomplete in one respect. The legislative grasshoppers are not allowed to chink and hop at will, under the contempt of the silent cattle; but they are honored and made notorious by the notice which they do not deserve. It was while he was defending himself and fellows against an impending law, that I first heard Herr Hasselmann in the tribune.

The Socialist leader is a young, almost boyish-looking man, with long hair falling over his shoulders in a romantic, poetical style. He dresses with the modesty becoming a representative of what he calls the *Canaille*. His oratory is dreary enough. Although he reads his harangue from manuscript or copious notes, and hurls at the house plenty of his blood-thirsty epigrams, his delivery is so tame and pointless that he rarely makes any impression. When he reaches his long finger out at the placid country members, the effect is far from striking. As a speaker, he is less vigorous than Bebel, and less authoritative than Hasenclever. But these two make short and abrupt appeals, while the man of sustained speech, of fatal prolixity, is Herr Hasselmann.

As we have given a specimen of this gentleman's newspaper writing, it is necessary to give also a specimen of his parliamentary efforts. The very speech above mentioned will serve our purpose as well as any other. The speaker had mentioned certain social evils which the Socialists oppose, and he continued :

"That we brand these things is awkward for certain persons, who cannot throw stones, because they themselves live in glass houses ; and who represent us as traveling agitators, with a club in one hand, and a bottle of petroleum in the other. To describe the red republic, communism, and atheism as our secret programme, this is possible only to a police agent, or to a writer on the subsidized press. If, on the one hand, you prosecute atheism, and, on the other hand, make Falk laws, you will find yourselves not on the golden middle way, but at the parting of the ways. Let every man save himself, in his own way, as Frederic the Great, himself an atheist, did. We do not sow evil in the present society, as the minister alleged, but we bring the evil to the knowledge of the people, and no penal code will prevent us from continuing to do that in the future. When the minister speaks of officials and teachers, on whom the Socialistic theories exercise a pernicious influence, his remark reflects not only his fears, but, also, an indirect acknowledgment of the truth of those theories. This fear, and this recognition, are very flattering for us, and we accept the compliment. The words which the Minister repeated, that the English laborers seek to make their ill condition better, while the Germans must first be convinced that their condition is ill, were uttered thirteen years ago by Lassalle. At that time they were justified; to-day they are not. As the Minister to-day spoke of bringing out cannon, it was openly a far greater and more serious appeal to the laboring classes, than any Socialist agitator, in a people's club, ever attempted. You may adopt the pending measure, or not: we shall continue to work and fight for Socialistic ideas with the same energy as in the past."

This speech, which was very long, and of which this extract is only the closing paragraph, was calmly received by the house, and only one or two of the more violent passages caused slight murmurs. But the Minister, Count Eulenburg, who is referred to so often by Hasselmann, thought it deserved a special reply. His second speech contained such a tribute to Hasselmann himself, and to the paper which Hasselmann edits, that an extract from that will contribute to the characterization of our hero. Hasselmann had been followed by Lasker, who took the Liberal ground, that the Socialistic principles were false and dangerous, but they ought to be combatted by education and enlightenment, rather than by repressive statutes. Against this "ideal standpoint," the Minister of the Interior felt bound to protest. "How can you compare the effect of such a remedy with the effect created when Herr Hasselmann, from this tribune, or in a popular assembly, holds a two hours' speech? Thither goes a crowd, which hardly know how to follow a line of thought, and comes away with excited feelings, and the conviction: We have heard our evangelist, and we are ready to suffer death for the ideas that the speaker has set forth. And the press of these gentlemen, the Socialistic journals, and pamphlets, and poems, they all find their way into the houses, into the families, into the work-shops of the laborers, and no other writings are read. The cabman must read his *Social-Democrat*, by day, and the working-man, when he comes home at night, cries out: 'Where is my *Social-Democrat?* I must learn how I am to conduct myself at my work.' In all these circles, only this Socialistic sheet is read, and by it the readers swear."

The Prussian minister is by no means a skilful artist, but this picture is tolerably faithful. At least it errs more from incompleteness of detail, than from an excess of color. In his argument for repressive legislation, against two evils that he deplores, the Minister, of course, only repeated with moderate force the venerable arguments of the Conservative guardians of society. In fact, any Liberal could retort that the Minister is less concerned about how the "crowd" acquire political principles, than what they acquire. If they read only orthodox sheets, and carried home from their meetings only sound Conservative views, the government might not stop to inquire whether they thought out those views themselves, or whether they accepted them on the authority of their single orthodox paper, and their favorite conservative orator. The friends of an impartial and independent press, of a Liberal political enlightenment, the Prussian Government and Count von Eulenburg have notoriously never been. The argument that the workingmen read with implicit faith only their one Socialistic sheet, instead of studying all sides, and by reflection reaching an enlightened opinion, was, therefore, a piece of special pleading.

But it is open to Liberals to advance such an argument, not only against the venerable reactionaries, who read only their *Kreuz-Zeitung*, but also against the children of toil, who must satisfy their intellectual hunger with such food as Herr Hasselmann daily sets before them. In the obligation to read such literature lies one of the hardest of the burdens of the workingman. It is not enough that the writer perverts the political reason of his readers; he also depraves their literary taste. They acquire a dislike for serious thinking, for positive political principles, by being taught that politics consist in the negation of all existing institutions, and the frantic repetition of formulas which have no sense. In this sort of teaching, as has been said above, and shown by example, Herr Hasselmann is a master.

I do not affirm that he is a willful impostor. It is possible, and indeed probable, that he is morally sincere, that he himself, not less than his unfortunate readers, is deceived by his own sounding phrases. A very young man, leaving his studies just at the time when they were beginning to mellow and discipline his mind, he sailed out upon a sea of treacherous verbiage, without the slightest logical experience to guide his course. To-day, he, doubtless, influences more readers than any other journalist in Germany. He appears to be, and probably is in person, a very harmless character, and cannot realize what a fatal service he does his eager clients. What he has been in the past he will continue to be in the future. In case of any violent disorders in the State, Hasselmann may be heard of in more serious work; but in the immediate future he will continue to proclaim his fiery generalities in his newspaper, and occasionally from the floor of the *Reichstag*.

XV.

HERR SONNEMANN.

U P to this point, our list of biographies includes leaders or representatives of every important party in German politics. The reader will observe that we have spoken interchangeably of the Prussian *Landtag*, or Diet, and the *Reichstag*, or Imperial Parliament, and, if this had been a treatise on politics, instead of on political leaders, a certain degree of confusion might have ensued. In fact, of course, the divisions, if not the proportions of parties, are the same in the one legislature as in the other. The fraction called "Alsatians," made up of the delegation from the two annexed provinces, is, of course, found only in a German Parliament; and the "Social-democrats," who now and then are carried into the *Reichstag*, on the shoulders of universal suffrage, are less successful for the Prussian House, which is chosen by indirect election. And, as the ministers in Germany are not required, as in England, to sit as members of Parliament, some of the characters are not even deputies. Our aim has been to sketch, in a measure, the nature of party relations in the new Empire, and the men who, whether they be deputies or ministers, or neither, are, in any sense, characteristic of those relations. At this point, therefore, it may be expedient to make a brief recapitulation.

The leading party in Germany is the National Liberal, which, in the *Reichstag*, has 148 members. Its importance has been honored in the names of Bennigsen, Simson, and Lasker. Some further characters will also be depicted from its ranks. The next party in strength, as represented in the *Reichstag* by 94 members, is that of the Ultramontanes. Its representative in these pages, Windthorst, is also its recognized leader. The party of progress, the *Fortschritts Partei*, to which belong Loewe, Schulze, and Jacoby, numbers in the same house no less than 49 seats. The party called sometimes the "German Party," and sometimes "Free Conservatives," has 31 members. With it may be reckoned Prince Hohenlohe, and the Ministers Dr. Falk and Camphausen, and, perhaps, Prince Bismarck himself. Count Harry von Arnim, though not now a deputy, aspired to become the leader of the Old Conservatives. The foregoing character, Hasselmann, we have taken for the Socialistic fraction. Two groups, or as the Germans say, *fractions*, the Poles and the Alsatians, stand for special, not to say, hopeless causes, but have no general political significance. The former vote, on most questions, with the Ultramontanes, and in parliamentary calculations are generally reckoned with them; and the same is true of the Alsatians, who, however, seldom appear in their places. Finally there is half a score of deputies who, declining to join any group, almost make a group by themselves. There is a sort of Irish logic, perhaps, which will be readily pardoned, in ranging under the party leaders Herr Sonnemann, who belongs to no party, and represents no opinion but his own.

Those opinions are indeed shared, or may be supposed to be shared, and it is to be hoped intelligently, by his constituents; but they have not yet formed a visible party. They may, doubtless, be gathered from the files of the *Frankfurter Zeitung*, which Sonnemann owns and edits. Or, if more formal expositions are desired, the student would be forced to read the innumerable pamphlets which Sonnemann has written and published, as well as the copious speeches that he has made in the *Reichstag*, in popular meetings, and elsewhere. Neither reticence nor indolence is one of this deputy's faults. It is a lucky, or an unlucky, session of the *Reichstag* which passes without a speech from him. As a member of the municipal councils of his city, Frankfort on the Main, as well as of many unions, and leagues, and associations, he has ample opportunities for his eloquence, even when the *Reichstag* is not sitting. But his great organ of communication with the public, is his newspaper, the *Frankfurter Zeitung*.

Leopold Sonnemann was born on the 29th of October, 1831, at Hochberg, in Lower Franconia, Bavaria. His parents were Hebrews. He studied at a commercial school, and then pursued a course of private instruction, after which he became a merchant. In 1856, he purchased the *Neue Frankfurter Zeitung*, which he converted into the *Frankfurter Zeitung*, and has since personally conducted.

It is now, in respect to circulation and influence, one of the most important journals in South Germany. It is well written, its correspondence is full and authentic, and although it is so peculiarly the personal organ of Herr Sonnemann, it is thoroughly independent, and enjoys the respect even of those who do not agree with its opinions. Although it is a great success, in a journalistic sense, it would appear that to Herr Sonnemann it was chiefly valuable as a vehicle for his peculiar theories. He, himself, pays more particular attention to social and economical questions. But, during the sessions of the *Reichstag*, when he is at Berlin, he sends regular political correspondence and leading articles.

Herr Sonnemann is classed by the government journals as a Social-democrat, but the *Frankfurter Zeitung* is wholly different from the *Volksstaat*, for instance, or the organ of Herr Hasselmann's revolutionary agitation. The *Volksstaat* or the *Neuer Social Democrat* is what a German with a slight sense of humor might call a *Fachblatt*. It has a specialty. Its object is the reform and regeneration of society, and it pays general politics only a general attention. Not so, the Radical journal at Frankfort on the Main. With it, the case is almost reversed. It is Radical in a general way, but political in the most detailed and especial sense of the word. The original Socialists like Hasselmann, look on political machinery as a clumsy evil, which circumstances force them to use for the propagation, if not for the realization of their more imposing theories. Sonnemann, on the contrary, respects the principle of civil government, and makes social reform, and political reform mutually serviceable the one to the other.

The latter, for instance, was no enemy of the principle of German unity, and. hardly of the imperial form, which that unity took. But he had strong views on the details of imperial organization. A member of the constituent *Reichstag*, he took an active part in the debates on the constitution ; and, after nearly all his amendments had been rejected, he voted against the new charter, as finally adopted by the House. On many collateral questions, too, he opposed the government. He was one of the little band which resisted the forcible annexation of Alsace-Lorraine, and which, by its energetic but fruitless defense of the right of these provinces themselves to be consulted, showed the recreant Liberalism of the majority. A free thinker and a hater of the Catholic priesthood, he nevertheless opposed on abstract grounds most of the imperial legislation in the *Culturkampf.* Thus he voted against the act for the expulsion of the Jesuits and affiliated societies ; and also against the act to punish certain pulpit offenses. Such measures he regarded as intrusions on personal rights, and as committing the new empire to the old reactionary doctrines on the press and the platform. In company with his friends he proposed, as is said above, a number of radical motions. They were, for instance, for the re-introduction of the German fundamental laws of 1849 ; for the total abolition of the salt tax ; for the separation of the Church from the State, and the schools from the Church. These were all promptly and unceremoniously rejected by the House. That he is not an irreconcilable, however, is shown by his course on the mint and currency bill, which he actively supported, in the main, according to the views or the government.

In appearance Herr Sonnemann looks anything but the Radical agitator. A large, portly man, with whiskers like Lord Dundreary, he dresses with a neatness and elegance quite un-Teutonic; and, on promenade, might pass for a gentleman of the world, and of leisure. His whiskers and his toilet are fine subjects for those brilliant Conservative caricaturists, who do not conceive that a man may be a gentleman in society, and yet a Radical in politics. But he is not a fop in Parliament, nor a *dilettante* in debate. He is not popular among his colleagues, for every man's hand is commonly against one who is thoroughly isolated in his views; and when he is speaking, smiles and sneers, and even stronger signs of dislike, are abundant. But these do not intimidate him. Although he sits in a remote corner of the hall, whither the majority has banished Socialists and other outcasts, he easily asserts his rights and defends his opinions. His strong masculine voice fills the large hall, and in spite of grave acoustical defects, reaches the most remote galleries. His sentences are terse and incisive, his enunciation clear, and his general delivery forcible and impressive. It must be said, however, that his manner is not conciliatory; it often encourages, not to say justifies, the aversion of the House. He has a habit of hissing his words contemptuously out between his teeth. It may be imagined that the impression of superciliousness, thereby created, does not conciliate the favor of a House, never patient with the Social democracy, or with any form of advanced Radicalism.

Outside of Parliament Sonnemann has long been an active and effective agitator. Within the limits of German law and police regulations, perhaps no living reformer has attended more congresses and other meetings, made a greater number of popular harangues, and in general conducted a more persistent campaign in favor of his own ideas. He was one of the founders of the "People's Economic Congress," which met every year to discuss in a popular way the leading questions of production, trade, commerce, etc., and he held for many years the position of President of the Section on Banking. In 1862, he was also one of the organizers of the "League of German Workingmen's Unions," which lasted till 1869. He took an active part in the agitation for a treaty of commerce with France, and for tariff reform in general. In the interest of this movement, he made a tour of Germany and appeared in numerous congresses, conventions, and meetings. Since he has been a member of the municipal council he has occupied himself more particularly with questions of taxation and finance, and his authority is willingly conceded, even by his political enemies. His efforts have been intelligently directed to lessening the burdens of the poorer. Many of the charitable and benevolent institutions of Frankfort owe themselves to his initiative. I may mention, for instance, the "Mechanics' Fund," "The Sustenance and Relief Union," "The Building and Savings' Union," and others. He has been active in promoting all public improvements, especially such as are of a popular character. Such are the Palm Garden at Frankfort, and the new Opera House. Above all must be mentioned the "Frankfort Union for Relief and Succor upon the Battle Field," which was so efficient during the French war. It raised two hundred thousand florins, which were personally disbursed on the field by Sonnemann and the other directors.

Any one who knows the immense importance granted to, and the immense influence exercised by trades unions and workingmen's clubs in Germany, will be able to gather, from the above account of Herr Sonnemann's connections some idea of his authority with the poor industrial classes of the community. It will be seen that he occupies a position, in many respects, midway between Schulze-Delitzsch and the Socialists, Hasselmann, Liebknecht, and others. He does not, like the former, confine himself to the useful but prosaic maxims of Dr. Franklin. He does not, like the latter, poison the workingmen with subversive theories, at the cost of their more substantial interests. The reforms which he has carried through seem to comprise both a system of political instruction and a system of popular economy. Prodigality was, indeed, never a vice of German workingmen. Only their economy lacked method, and they had never learned the secret of lawful combination for the lawful and peaceful exercise of all their resources in their own cause. Schulze first taught them a salutary system on a national scale, but their benefactor and champion, in Frankfort, is Herr Sonnemann.

It must be said, however, that Herr Sonnemann's influence is chiefly local. He is a Jew, and the City of Frankfort on the Main has a larger ratio of Jews than any other in Germany. The traveler who spends a day there, and reads his Baedeker or Murray, will learn that, in the middle ages, the Hebrews were assigned to certain limits outside of the walls, beyond which they were forbidden to trespass: and the guide, if one be taken, will point out the forced retreat of the heretics. That state of things has, however, long passed away. The Jews have not only fought their own way to all the privileges of the city, but they have practically become masters of their former oppressors. Not only do they control the commerce, the banking, the finance of Frankfort, but the conduct of municipal affairs, and the expression of the city's voice in national politics, is also, in a great measure, in their hands. These facts alone, however, do not explain Sonnemann's position. The Jews who control the trade and banking and the municipal affairs, are capitalists, and capital in Frankfort, as elsewhere, is conservative. But the first virtue of the Jews is prudence. The city contains, also, a large and turbulent Radical and Democratic element, and the only way to hold this in check is to aid it in electing the least objectionable of its favorites. Herr Sonnemann holds sound views on financial questions; a man of means, he also has material interests at stake, and the control of a powerful journal makes him a grand local dignitary. The policy may not proceed from very lofty political convictions, but it saves the old free city from a Hasselmann or a Bebel.

PART VI.

THE SCHOLAR IN POLITICS.

XIV.

Professor Gneist.

PROFESSOR GNEIST is a person of whom it is the fashion to speak with respect, if not with affection. One of the most concrete individuals in German public life, he nevertheless exists for the mass of the people as some shadowy but mighty abstraction, a power which is known to be, but is seldom felt. What the Hindoo said of his idol, may be said of Dr. Gneist: "We feel that he is ugly, but we know that he is great." He has one of those peculiar faces which do not frighten children or attract adults; for it is perfectly neutral in expression, and suggests all mental qualities, chiefly because it reveals none. It has been cleverly said of some American lawyer, that he is much esteemed in England on account of his supposed reputation in America, and much esteemed in America on account of his supposed reputation in England. Dr. Gneist's fame is of this indirect and intangible nature. Schultze respects him, because Müller has read his book on "Juries;" and Müller admires him, on the strength of

Schultze's opinion of "English Public Law." He is an aggregate power which cannot be analyzed. He is an intellectual potentate; but, while the fact of his sway is always present and undisputed, it is impossible to discover the details on which it rests.

It cannot, indeed, be said that his opportunities of influence and power are few or unsubstantial. He has sounded almost all the depths and shoals of honor in these great branches of the public service. He has ascended the judicial ladder, as far as the *Ober-Tribunal;* the academic ladder, as far as a university rectorship; and the parliamentary ladder, to the *Reichstag*. More recently, he has become president of the highest disciplinary court in the very bureaucracy which he once so bitterly attacked.

Rudolph Gneist, doctor of laws, regular professor in the faculty of jurisprudence at the University of Berlin, was born on the 13th of August, 1816. After the usual course of study at the gymnasium and university, he adopted the profession of law, and, in 1833, became *Auscultator*. In 1841, he was *Assessor* before the Superior Court or "Chamber," and 1846, assistant judge in the Supreme Tribunal. This post, and with it the judicial career, he abandoned in 1850, in part from a preference for academical work, in part for political reasons. Already, in 1839, he was a *privat-docent* in law; in 1844, professor; in 1872–74, rector and pro-rector. His parliamentary career may be said to have begun in 1848, with a seat in the Municipal Council, which he still retains. From 1858 to the present time, he has been a member of the Prussian Lower House; in the Imperial Parliament he has sat from the first. Of unofficial positions which he holds or has held, may be mentioned the Chairmanship of the German Jurists' Association (1869) ; he has been President of the Union for Social Science at Eisenach (1872) ; President of the Central Union for the Working Classes ; Chairman of the Scientific Union, of the Singing Academy, etc., etc. In the House of Deputies (Prussian) he sits for a district in the province of Saxony ; in the *Reichstag* he is elected from the district of Landeshut. In his earlier days he belonged to the so-called " Fraction Vincke ;" later he was leader of the Left Centre, and, at present, is classed with the National Liberals.

The participation of Gneist in the Liberal movements of 1848, was active and resolute. So prominent was he, that he won the disfavor of the government ; and many petty and some serious obstacles were put in the way of his professional progress. In the sketch of Jacoby, there is some account of the royal plan to adjourn the National Assembly to Brandenburg. Dr. Gneist was not then in Parliament, but he took part in a vigorous and novel extra-parliamentary protest against the plan. The Prince of Prussia, at that time heir apparent, now the reigning king, was supposed to have great influence with his brother. He was a stringent defender of prerogative ; a bold, stern, and fearless soldier, and an object of intense popular aversion. When the extraordinary purpose of the king was made known, people at once recognized the hand of Prince William. A deputation was accordingly appointed to wait upon him. Dr. Gneist was its leader and spokesman. He made, or began, a long address upon the subject of his mission, when the prince interrupted him, and declared that the speech had not convinced him that the king was wrong in his treatment of the National Assembly. It is said that he threw his sword upon the table, like Gallus in the Roman legend, and said, that if he were king, he would write his throne-speeches with that.

In obedience to the same principles, Dr. Gneist undertook the defence of those accused of participation in the outbreak of March, 1848. One remark that he made at the time has become famous. The attorney for the government had mentioned that many of those who fell in the movement were released or escaped criminals, and that the death of such was no loss to society. Gneist replied: "Such a death restored them their honor." A year later, in 1849, to defend the jury system against the attacks which its great services for freedom of speech and press were bringing upon it, he published his treatise, to which reference has been made above. The so-called *Juristentag*, or annual convention of jurists, was not liked by the government. It was generally attended by great numbers of Liberal lawyers and professors, and by judges, and upon these latter an inhibition was placed. They were forbidden to take part in the proceedings. Soon after the promulgation of this order, Dr. Gneist retired from the bench.

Professor Gneist is a popular holiday speaker, and the frequent demands upon him have, perhaps, contributed to give him an oracular, not to say bombastic, style of speech. Funeral orations, dedicatory orations, toast responses, these are not supposed to exact too much thought from the performer, and, in a man of Dr. Gneist's reputation, they encourage even more vicious tendencies. An example of this will be found in a speech made by him on taking the chair at a public meeting in Berlin. An English meeting had voted sympathy with the ecclesiastical policy of Prince Bismarck, and the citizens of the Prussian capital met to return thanks. Dr. Gneist began by saying that a "most respectable assembly, such as the beautiful festival halls of the capital have seldom seen, holds it to be a duty to make a grateful answer to the recent warm expression of English sympathy for the German Emperor and the German People. A similar pulsation went through both nations long before the days of Waterloo; it is a deep feeling for freedom of conscience and freedom of thought, a feeling which is not able to separate science and conscience. We may accept the expression of this sympathy in the consciousness that the German Emperor and the German People, in the present conflict, have deserved it. No nation of the earth has endured so much, in hard, prolonged struggles for freedom of conscience as the German, until she reached the conclusion that, for the two great Churches there must be room enough on God's earth."

This was what is called a gala occasion, and Professor Gneist would naturally try, in his effort, to justify his choice for the honor of president. Yet there are in this very opening two grave errors, one of inference or suggestion, and one of fact. It is an error to assume that the pending struggle of the State in Germany against the Catholic Church is a struggle for "freedom of conscience." It is a second and far graver error to say that Germany has suffered more for freedom of conscience than any other, or, to use his own language, than "any" nation. It is not so easy to erase from the pages of history the Huguenots of France, the Hussites of Bohemia, the Puritans of England, and, above all, the immortal patriots and martyrs of Netherlands. One does not of course expect in a popular harangue the severe logic of a written treatise; but Dr. Gneist is a professor of political science, and is, moreover, famous for pruning the periods of young orators.

It is but just, however, to say that Dr. Gneist has or had a certain force of epigrammatic expression, and that many of his terse remarks were taken up by the people and have passed into history. One, and perhaps the most familiar, concerned the bureaucracy of Prussia. When somebody remarked in his presence that the March Revolution of 1848, was a failure because it stopped short of the throne, Professor Gneist replied: "No! It was a failure because it left the old Prussian bureaucracy untouched." In fact it did not leave the bureaucracy quite intact. The system has undergone no insignificant modifications within thirty years, and of all these, the events of 1848 were the historic condition, if not the cause. But the remark of Dr. Gneist nevertheless hinted at the real tyrant in the original Prussian system; and gave pointed expression to the hatred with which the people then regarded the oligarchy of clerks and copyists. No man knew that system better than he. Not only had he studied it profoundly, and from all sides—practical, political, social; but he had also studied with equal care a system quite the reverse,—that of England. His book on the administrative system of England, which was both analytical and historical, has many faults which critics have not spared. It has been said that the execution of the work does not quite correspond to the confidence and authority of the author. It was not only easy, but for a German almost necessary, that in collecting great masses of useless erudition he should often miss the essential point, the interpreting idea, the logical secret, without which there is no progress; and thus, while this great work is of value as a formal sketch of the English administrative system, it adds but little to that knowledge, so imperfect in foreigners, of the philosophy of Anglo-Saxon institutions.

A year since there was a report that Dr. Gneist would visit America, and subject the American system to similar treatment. Whether the report was false—whether it was true at the time, and the plan has since been abandoned—or whether the journey will eventually be made and the book written, is not yet clear. But if the eminent jurist should honor us with his visit, and our government with his researches, the result would be an exhaustive collection of facts, and the enunciation of many principles, which, as the fruit of a few months' residence, would be very edifying to American schools.

There are other phrases by Dr. Gneist, but little less famous. One of these was his glowing "appeal from the government to the conscience of the State," from the organized and contemptuous ministerial persecution of liberal men and measures, to the higher reason of an educated and conscientious commonwealth. On another occasion, he publicly branded the policy of Bismarck with the stigma of Cain. It was during the struggle of the *Landtag*, or the Lower House of the *Landtag*, against the unconstitutional course of king and ministers. Dr. Menzel describes the incident. A proposition was made by the deputy von Bonin to smooth the way to a compromise; but, since it recognized the organization of the army, demanded only a slight reduction in its strength, and above all settled the

Landwehr question in a sense contrary to that of the majority, while the war minister himself spoke of it only with reserve, the House rejected it. The member who reported the measure from the committee back to the House, Dr. Gneist, closed his speech on the 5th of May, in the following words: "The minister of war is not only a political, he is also a religious man; and for that reason, he will believe me, that the re-organization, with Cain's mark of perjury on its forehead, will be no permanent institution of the country, as long as there be such a thing as divine justice." The minister, Count von Roon, answered: "When the reporter permitted himself to attack me personally, in a way unheard of in Parliament, I was astonished that he was not called to order. But I must remark that the words of the speaker carry on their forehead the mark of exaggeration and shamelessness." The President of the Chamber interposed, Gneist disclaimed the intention to insult the minister personally, and von Roon withdrew his observations. The *mot* of Gneist nevertheless went through the land. So cleverly and forcibly did it press the popular feeling toward the army bill, that no one stopped to analyze it, and inquire whether the "brand of Cain" was that of perjury, and whether a military re-organization could have a "forehead." Indeed the two infuriated speakers seem to have carried on a battle of bad rhetoric as well as of ugly insinuations; and though the war minister won the case by boldly giving a "forehead" to Gneist's words, the credit of introducing that striking figure must be given to his opponent.

The last occasion on which I had the honor of hearing Dr. Gneist in public, was at the dedication of the monument to the memory of Stein, at Berlin. The orator stands only in an intellectual relation to the great reformer. Stein's biography, a monument of literary labor, was composed by other hands. But of all modern Prussian statesmen, Dr. Gneist is perhaps the leading representative, as well in practical politics as in political speculation, of that great man's ideas, and achievements. No two persons could differ more than Stein and his eulogist. The former was a man of genius, the latter is only a man of robust understanding. The former deduced schemes of reform from a profound study of the evils of existing society; the latter is only a man of expedients, learned from the observation of other societies. The one was bold, original, showy, brilliant. The other is prosaic, heavy, and commonplace. Stein had a quickness of perception and a fertility of resource, which swept away the dull courtiers who came in his path. Dr. Gneist is a doctrinaire, who ennobles obvious truths by an artificial gravity of manner. In spite of all these differences between the two, Dr. Gneist was still the best fitted to do justice to the character of Stein's work, if not of Stein himself; and some passages from his eulogy will give an idea of this gentleman at his best.

The translation is that of the correspondent of the *London Times:*

"The likeness of our great statesman gravely looks down upon the spot once trodden by him. What a contrast between these modern days and that stormy October, 1807, in which Baron von Stein was recalled to office to direct the affairs of this monarchy! Prematurely aged, enfeebled, and torn, the kingdom of Frederick the Great lay at the feet of a haughty conqueror, when Stein conceived the idea of regenerating it by emancipating the people, There was little courage and less energy left, when Stein uttered these weighty words—'To lift up a people it is necessary to give liberty, independence, and property to its oppressed classes, and extend the protection of the law to all alike. Let us emancipate the peasant, for free labor alone sustains a nation effectually. Restore to the peasant the possession of the land he tills, for the independent proprietor alone is brave in defending hearth and home. Free the citizen from monopoly and the tutelage of the bureaucracy, for freedom in workshop and town-hall has given to the ancient burgher of Germany the proud position he held. Teach the land-owning nobles that the legitimate rank of the aristocracy can be maintained only by disinterested service in county and state, but is undermined by exemption from taxes and other unwarrantable privileges. If the political functions formerly held by the Estates of the Realm are now vested in the bureaucracy, and the latter order has thus become one of the most important in the kingdom, it is all the more necessary to free it from its inherent defects. Instead of confining itself to pedantic book knowledge, and esteeming red tape and salary above everything else, the bureaucracy should study the people, live with the people, and adapt its measures to the living realities of the times.' Thus thought the Baron of the Holy Roman Empire, thus acted the Prussian Minister of State. No German statesman has ever so thoroughly relied upon the action of a free and united people as Stein; no one was more keenly alive to the beneficial effect of freedom in the innermost recesses of home, in the work of the State, and in the creed of the Church. He regarded monarchy as a means of educating and elevating a nation, of increasing and developing every noble and manly feature of their character. He vindicated religion as the only true basis of moral life, and he looked upon an army raised by universal subscription as a school in which honor, discipline, and love of country were to be inculcated and practically applied. 'Elevate, unite, and combine,' he said, 'the various classes of this regenerated people. Accustom the nation to devote themselves with all their heart to public affairs, and believe that sensual pleasures, idleness, and the love of gain and riches can never be effectually counteracted, except by patriotism and the love of one's neighbor. Constitutional forms are a matter of comparative indifference as long as liberty exists. To elect public officers is one method of dealing with public affairs. Not the election, however, but daily participation in the affairs of the State is the principal thing. Upon this daily participation the new constitution of Germany must be based.' The man to whom we are indebted for these teachings was not a man of words, but of deeds—deeds founded upon a character full of patriotism, energy, truth, and faith. Deeply imbued with the fear of God, and therefore free from all fear of man, aiming at great objects, and never hesitating to pursue them in the teeth of all difficulties, he frequently contented himself with laying down principles, leaving their execution and the cautious choice of ways and means to others. Full of noble indignation against fear and diffidence, selfishness and false appearances; haughty, abrupt and imperious, where these qualities were required; he boldly warred against prejudice and obsolete customs. It was a merciful provision of Providence that this noble Stein, this precious stone and gem of our unity, was a rough diamond, preserving in his character the rigor and vigor indispensable in the reformer. If the political institutions created by him have been successful, this is chiefly owing to the indomitable force of his convictions, which, reflected in the laws enacted by him, within a couple of years infused a fresh vitality into the national mind. When the hour of liberty struck, Stein banished the foreigner, became the herald of war, the admonisher of the council, and by his fiery enthusiasm incited his wrathful countrymen to pursue the conqueror from the borders of Siberia to the River Seine. He experienced a triumph worth living for. He, too, stayed long enough in our midst to witness that doubtful period in which the various classes of the reconstituted nation, amid sundry changes and agitations, tried to shake down into their new places. He departed when the struggle was waxing warm, and when the ideas sown by him for the identification of people and State began to penetrate the crust of prejudice and error which had so long hidden and choked their growth. Prussia, to whom he devoted a life's labors, has at last fulfilled the wishes of Stein and the hopes of the nation by restoring unity and solidity to Germany. It having been our happy lot to realize what he died too early to witness, this solemn day intimately connects us with him. In this inaugural hour, we need not recount the tale of his life ; it is part and parcel of German history. Nor need we rejoice at having a monument to remind us of the departed statesman ; all the institutions of modern Germany bear the impress of his mind. Neither do we wish to boast of this monument as a symbol of glory. The very idea of glory was utterly abhorrent to his pure soul, to all he wrote and did. Like our own glorious emperor and king, the leading minister of Frederick William III. had a right to say :— 'We have not sought, though we have found glory and power in defending our dearest possessions and upholding the legitimate claims of the nation. Glory and honor be to God alone!' No, as the inscription tells us in the most unpretending language, this is no monument of glory, but of gratitude ; no monument of victory, but of thankfulness. This debt of gratitude has been long delayed. It is now many years since the talented sculptor of this statue departed this life. For years we have been looking for a site in this city, which, like the people to whom it appertains, has long been busy in fulfilling every-day duties before putting on holiday costume in honor of the accumulated result. The great deceased will forgive our tardy tribute. He never thought of his own monument, but only of the *Monumenta Germaniæ.**

" We thank God that after many a hard struggle, the successor of Stein's sovereign, the German Emperor and King, through the illustrious heir of the German Empire, does honor to the memory of Baron von Stein. We are elated by the thought that the statue we unveiled amid festive hymns records the vow that our sons will preserve by labor, faithfulness and obedience what their fathers have created 'with God for King and Country.' I trust that the Stein Monument will remind this city and coming generations of the foundation on which our history is built."

Dr. Gneist seems now to have reached the age when a struggle against the government for abstract principles has no more pleasure for him. During the late debate on the

---

* The famous collection of the mediæval and ancient records of Germany ; a work suggested by Stein and carried out by his biographer, Dr. Pertz.

amendment to the Penal Code he was a silent listener. By accepting the presidency of the "Administrative Court" he seems to have made his peace with that bureaucracy which he once so bitterly denounced, and to have settled back into a dignified conservative repose.

XV.

PROFESSOR VIRCHOW.

THIS gentleman is doubtless better known abroad than his friend, Dr. Gneist, but not as a politician. The author or discoverer of the cellular system of physiology is now known wherever medicine is a science, and professional zeal a virtue. It is equally necessary to make him known to men who care nothing about the cellular physiology, but like to pay tribute to the brave citizen, the unimpeachable politician. For Dr. Virchow is another one of those bold "tribunes of the people" who, in their youthful days, enjoyed the ill will of princes and suffered persecution for their honest opinions. Nay, he is a scholar whose researches were interrupted by a reactionary minister, a teacher whose labors were suspended because he had political principles. He had to meet, and he met successfully, one of the hardest of all trials. He had to purchase an academic position, and the opportunity to pursue the study of a profession to which he was passionately devoted, by renouncing opinions which no law forbade a Prussian subject to hold, or else retire from Berlin and become an exile, with a stigma of disgrace affixed by the King of Prussia. He chose the latter course, and enriched the annals of his country by one more example of conspicuous civic courage.

Rudolph Virchow was born on the 13th of October, 1821, at Schievelbein, in the province of Pomerania. After the usual course at the nearest gymnasium, that of Cöslin, he began his university studies at Berlin, and graduated with honors. In 1843, he was appointed assistant physician, and later *Prosector* in the Berlin hospital *Charité*. His principal was the great surgeon and physician, Schönlein. This brilliant practitioner, and equally brilliant lecturer, was a complete despot in his professional authority, and many stories have been told of his summary treatment even of royal patients; but to young Virchow he early took a great liking. The patronage of Schönlein was of immense advantage to him, and his progress was sufficiently rapid until his political opinions began to attract the attention of the government. About this time he became acquainted and formed also a professional connection with Reinhardt. Not only did the two friends pursue together their pathological investigations, but they also published together the results of those investigations in the so-called *Archives for Pathological Anatomy and Physiology* — a medical periodical of wide circulation. After Reinhardt's death, in 1852, Virchow continued the publication alone. In 1848, he aided Leubuscher to found a new medical periodical, *Die Medizinische Reform* — a periodical in which the most radical professional theories found expression. In 1846,

Virchow gave lectures at the University of Berlin, which were so numerously attended, that he was made professor in 1847. The next year he was sent, by the government, to Silesia, where a famine, the so-called *Hunger Typhus*, was causing widespread devastation. He was instructed at once to render medical aid and to make scientific observations. These latter he gave to the world immediately in a pamphlet, "Report over the Upper Silesian Hunger Typhus." In 1868, he published a farther work, "On Hunger Typhus."

The year 1848 came, and with it came decisive events in Virchow's history. The weakness, the timidity, the vacillation of Frederic William IV., had so often deceived the people that little confidence was placed in his loyalty, even on the momentous 18th of March, when he came out bareheaded upon the balcony of his palace, to announce to the angry and threatening assemblage that their legitimate demands would be granted. He had hardly made his appearance when two musket shots, fired by treachery or carelessness, changed, in an instant, the face of affairs. The people cried that they were betrayed; the king fled into his palace from the storm; the cry to arm and defend resounded through the city, and in two hours forty barricades were erected in the streets. These hasty barriers were manned not alone, as the reactionaries pretended, by workmen, vagabonds, and escaped criminals. Behind them, fought men of culture, talent, and promise; men who added to all other civic virtues that of profound political convictions; men who enjoyed the possession or the hope of honor and fame in the learned professions, and it is said that one of these was Dr. Rudolph Virchow. The report may be false. But it is certain that if he did not actually take part in the outbreak, his sympathies were with the people who tried, however unadvisedly, by that means to redress their grievances.

After this the young professor seems, at least, to have been a doomed man. At first, the government did not feel strong enough openly to dismiss so brilliant a teacher, and not till a year later, did the Minister of Education, Raumer, whose Liberal connections ought to have taught him more charity—not till Easter, 1849, did this minister venture to carry out the threatened measure. Even after this dismissal Virchow was temporarily re-instated, doubtless to invite a political recantation. But the trick failed. Thereupon, he was again dismissed; this time it was supposed definitively, and he accepted an invitation to Würtzburg in the faculty of medicine. Prussia had banished a radical politician, but she had also banished one of the rising scholars of the age.

To Würtzburg Virchow transferred not only his political opinions, but also his scientific and professional spirit. He now became one of the leading members of a faculty which, at that time, made the medical department of the university famous. The organs of this faculty, the medical society, and the published "Proceedings" of the same, were well known throughout Germany, and, indeed, to medical scholars, everywhere. The famous cellular pathology of Virchow was suggested by him at this time, though it was not carefully developed and explained till 1859. According to his theory, the essential cause of the modifications of the organs, and their disease, is the sensitiveness or irritableness of the cells. The great work in which he defended this theory has been translated into nearly every civilized language. In the United States, it is said that the Federal Government distributed a large number of copies among the surgeons and physicians of the army. Even without his political heresies, it is probable that Virchow would have been objectionable to a king who was such by divine right, and would not tolerate in his state the study of a godless Hegelianism. For the great pathologist was as radical in religion as in medicine and politics. "I do not deny the fact of spirit," he once said or wrote, "but for me there is only value in what I see." When there was no other complaint against him, it was always possible to adduce his "materialism," and unfortunately the King of Prussia and his minister of education had equally strong convictions on the subject.

As an exile and a stranger, it is probable that Virchow gave less attention to politics, while he was at Würtzburg. Not only was he withdrawn from the scene of party strife, but even at home, in Prussia, the democrats had taken no active part in public affairs after the triumph of reaction in 1850. By their abstention rather than by their opposition, they made their protest against the counter-revolution, and it mattered little to Virchow, whether he was in retirement at Würtzburg or in Berlin.

But it made a vast difference to the University of Berlin. The medical faculty, which at that time was not of the strongest, was much criticised by the professional journals, and the friends of the institution were impatient that the caprice of a fantastic prince and the bigotry of an unenlightened minister should deprive it of its most illustrious name. The reputation of Virchow had been steadily growing at Würtzburg. Already he was known and cited by scientific men all over the world ; and wherever he was known as a physicist, he was also known as an exile for conscience' sake. At last the pressure became too strong to be withstood. The same Räumer who had dismissed him ignominiously in 1849, was obliged to call him back in 1856, to give him his old position, but with added power and honors. Since that time he has been undisturbed. He is professor of pathology at the university, and director of microscopic experiments in the clinics at the *Charité*.

In 1862, Virchow became a member of the House of Deputies in the Prussian *Landtag*. His career as a deputy began, therefore, with that of Bismarck as a minister ; but in other respects there is not only no identity or concord between them, but rather fierce and bitter warfare. Virchow, if not one of the most formidable, is, at least, one of the most persistent and determined critics whom Bismarck has had to meet. I say, "if not formidable," because he is not a professional critic who may become a rival, who heads a party, conducts intrigues, and, in general, fights with the stubbornness and energy of a candidate for the succession ; but he is simply an active and zealous citizen who uses his parliamentary power as a means of serving his fellow-citizens. He is an independent critic, not a politician in control of a faction ; he is feared as a personal antagonist, but not as an ambitious politician.

At the same time, there are other circumstances which give Virchow unusual influence in the House. His brother deputies, for instance, must be impressed by the spectacle of the first pathologist in the world laying down microscope and dissecting knife at the command of an exalted public spirit, and taking part patiently in the dullest and heaviest debates. Learning thus to appreciate his unselfish patriotism, they argue from that to the soundness of his political judgment. This is a pardonable error, but still an error, for Virchow is not a leader whom it is safe blindly to follow. He is a *doctrinaire* and a Radical, and the records of the past twelve years will hardly show a single great measure conceived and carried through by him.

The Deputy Virchow has two grave faults. One of these is peculiar to men who have thought out their political convictions by abstract methods and as a recreation—to scholars and recluses who leave the closet for the forum—an offensive dogmatism, which takes too little account of the feelings and opinions of others. It does not follow, because one has discovered the cellular pathology, that one's political theories are above examination. The professor, most certainly, does not feel any such superiority, but his manner suggests it; hence his warmth too often leads him into intemperate language, or intolerant conduct, which is equally exasperating, and equally likely to provoke sharp replies and angry disputes. One of the most famous of these was with Bismarck himself.

It was on the 30th of May, 1865, during that protracted struggle between Bismarck and the House. The estimates for the navy had just been rejected. The Minister President remarked that the denial of any and every allowance for the fleet was in singular contrast to the zeal with which the Liberals had formerly pressed for a strengthening that arm of the service. Professor Virchow replied : "The project was not seriously meant ; it was only a feint. But it is a perversion of the truth to say that the committee had no interest in the marine. If the Minister President has read the report, then I do not know what I shall say of his honesty. The truth is that the reserves in the State Treasury are decreasing; that the means of carrying on the government without a budget are growing less, and that it is sought to restore the deficiency by a loan, in order to be able still to sit by warm stoves." The majority laughed, when Bismarck inquired where matters would end, if insults were uttered which demanded personal satisfaction; and he added to the House: "There is an opportunity for that, if it be agreeable to you." Virchow would not retract his words; the President would not call him to order. The next day Bismarck sent Virchow a challenge, which, of course, was not accepted. The political friends of the professor counseled him to decline, and he received many addresses of approval from the country. This incident caused a great sensation at the time, but it was nearly forgotten by the present generation, when it was cited, not long ago, in a singular way, in court. A gentleman was on trial for sending a challenge—a species of pleasure that the German laws have long denied, except to the military—and, in mitigation of sentence, the defendant referred to the case of Bismarck *versus* Virchow, and observed that Bismarck had never been prosecuted for his challenge. The judge replied that he was not prosecuted because he was protected by the military uniform which, as an officer in the *Landwehr*, he is accustomed and entitled to wear.

The second complaint against Virchow is that he speaks too often. He is never unreasonably long, and he is seldom dull or tiresome, but he has a fatal facility of speech, which he, too commonly, fails to control. Windthorst, who is by no means reticent, would call Virchow garrulous. He might write upon his battle-shield the motto, "Ever ready," but it could only be taken in the sense of ever willing. Ever prepared, in the sense of special equipment, by study and reflection, for the various special questions, as they come up in the House, he, unfortunately, is not; and, still more unfortunately, he does not always regard lack of preparation as a reason for silence. It is true that the special student who crams for particular subjects is often less useful, as a legislator, than the man of broad, general, available information. But the latter must know when his general information is adequate for the occasion, and when the more profound and exact knowledge of the specialist is to be invoked. This is a distinction which Virchow does not make. He is a frequent and copious speaker on questions which, involving general principles, may be familiar to all minds that have reflected on political subjects; he is a brilliant debater on problems to which his trained intellect has been fairly applied; but he also takes up with equal readiness, and settles with equal authority, issues on which more modest men, not specially prepared, would gladly be silent.

Even as I write this paragraph, an evening paper calls attention, though in a less friendly spirit, to this unfortunate tendency. The measure before the House was the new constitution for the Evangelical Church in Prussia, an ecclesiastical or politico-ecclesiastical subject, on which neither a professor of pathology, nor a Radical agitator, could be supposed to have any indispensable general views. It appears, too, that Dr. Virchow did not think it necessary to supply the want of previous information by special study. He plunged fearlessly and recklessly into the discussion, grappled with men who had given years of thought to such questions, and the result may be learned from the critic of the *Post*. He says, that "among the speakers who took part in the important general discussion of the bill upon the constitution of the Evangelical Church, Dr. Virchow was, without doubt, one of the least fortunate in his arguments. Aside from the fact that he made the mistake of treating a section of the bill that had been adopted by the Synod, as having been abandoned in the scheme accepted by the king, whereas it was only given a different place and form—aside from this, his reasoning was so weak that the Evangelical Church can only be pitied that she must see her affairs discussed and pronounced upon by one who has such an imperfect understanding of ecclesiastical questions. If Dr. Virchow pretends that 'the ecclesiastics who drew up the synodal scheme in question issued from the school which Stahl in politics, and Hengstenberg in theology, founded and represented,' it is a phrase which would perhaps make an impression on a ward meeting, but which, neither in the attitude of the General Synod nor of the Provincial Synods, has any justification in facts."*

So writes the critic of the Conservative and ministerial sheet, which is indeed politically hostile to Dr. Virchow. But the Berlin correspondent of a more pretentious periodical, the *Grenzboten*, which is more liberal than the *Post*, is scarcely less severe in its strictures:

"And now," it says, "followed Hero Virchow. He had

---

* *Die Post*, March 2, 1875.

armed himself in all his force, and whoever was present during the session of the 26th of February must say that this personage, as often as he has spoken, never before appeared so distinctly in his own character. At the outset, he declared to the House that no other entered upon the discussion so well prepared as he. As thereupon a laugh arose from the benches of the Conservatives, he held up the volume of debates of the General Synod, and demanded: 'Have you read that through ? I have studied it from beginning to end.' It was imposing. But when he had finished his discourse, the *Cultus-Minister* proved that he could, at most, only have glanced at the reports ; that all his deductions were false or unreasonable ; that he had not only not read the reports, but not even the synodal constitution."*

In spite of, or rather perhaps on account of, these adverse criticisms, the reader may demand from this now historical speech a specimen of Virchow's powers of declamation. I select the closing paragraph, in which he recapitulates his objections to the measure :

"And now in what concerns the *Summus Episcopus :* that is an institution which has remained by the side of the constitution, as it were, a forgotten magnate. Ever appears, when nothing else helps, the old king of 1849 and 1850. He plays the same part here as the war delegate of Herr von Bismarck, who regularly enters when there is no other salvation. That happens because old institutions, which ought to have been abolished, have been retained with the constitution. The monarchical power

---

* *Die Grenzboten*, 1876, No. 10, page 398.

always appears in spite of the constitution. The attempt to sustain a personal ecclesiastical authority has often been made by Prussian kings. But I have reached through my historical studies other results than those of the *Cultus-Minister* (minister of worship). After absolutism has been everywhere abolished, shall we restore it in the domain of ecclesiastical affairs? I am not an enthusiast for the constitutional principle in this domain. The constitutional principle was not introduced into the world to make churches; that, according to my conception, would soon put an end to our inner Protestant life. We should thereby introduce a Catholic tendency, and that we will not have. He who wishes that, may create the necessary organs, but he must not compel others to adopt them. The Protestant Union deceives itself, if it believes in the possibility of building a wall here. The organization of the General Synod cannot exist indifferently by the side of the civil institutions; irremediable confusion would be the result. A spiritual king by the side of a temporal one is inconceivable to us."

On special occasions, however, Professor Virchow is a felicitous and popular orator. I have mentioned the funeral orations of Dr. Gneist. He has a broader practical understanding and a better trained historical judgment; but Virchow has a deeper warmth of conviction, and a more active fancy. The former can make an admirable analysis of a character like Stein, for instance, which belongs to the past and is little affected by the passions and prejudices of the present. The latter is more successful when he throws the warmth of his feelings into the eulogy of a personal or a political friend. His discourse in honor of Schönlein, his friend and teacher, delivered in 1865, was widely admired, and among more recent performances may be mentioned the tribute to Hoverbeck.

This gentleman was a politician, and an extract from his eulogy will suit most nearly the character of this sketch, while giving an equally good idea of Virchow's style. After tracing Hoverbeck's career as a Prussian deputy, through the stormy *Confliktszeit*, he ushers him into the *Reichstag* as an imperial legislator, charged with still graver duties. "And yet," he concludes, "it was little that he ac-accomplished. In the main, he saw with anxiety into the future. The faulty organization of the empire, the conflict always growing and threatening between budget and army, occupied his spirit more than the progress that had been made in certain fields of legislation. Even the *Cultur-kampf* appeared to him in many of its phases to be a treacherous side-path, which led the people away from the broad thoroughfare; and, although we must recognize the conviction finally taking possession of him, that this conflict was an important step in the liberation of the people; although, with a heavy heart, he resolved to support exceptional measures in the *Reichstag*, it troubled him, nevertheless, that it was a political strife, undertaken and conducted on artificial grounds, and in no sense from a free and conscious insight into the moral necessity of freeing the citizen, with full enlightenment on the end to be obtained, and the purpose to obtain it. When he looked into politics, he saw everywhere new and greater work for himself. Everywhere uncleanness, incompleteness, irresolution—and yet he did not despair. Like every good man, he was inspired by the confidence of the people. He never wavered in the assurance that his German people would keep the resolution and the will to conquer all their rights. He never lost the confidence that, in spite of everything, the German Empire would be an empire of justice and progress. In this assurance, in this hope, he passed away. He had wandered out to the mountains, where freedom dwells. He would seek strength for new labors. But this was never more to be granted to him. He had done an abundant measure of work. * * * His place in Parliament will be filled by another; but his party, yes, his people, will always see it empty. The massive figure is broken. When it arose, towering upward, when there was seen in it the appearance of a man equal to himself, then every one who had a true heart and loved honest speech won confidence. Like the Polish peasant, who heard a speech by him and applauded without having understood a word—like him, everybody who looked into those calm eyes, and that manly face, so full of determination and spirit, knew that his conscience was as pure as gold, and his conclusions clear as the sun. The words which fell from his mouth were few, but they were sharp as a knife. Before him stood no screen of lies, no curtain of the truth. And yet there lay in that countenance the lines of moderation, of mildness, of benevolence, which opened hearts and announced his sympathy with all the good and true."

But when we have named his professor's chair and his deputy's seat, we have by no means exhausted the instruments with which Virchow works for the public good. If the best citizen be he who most actively concerns himself with the cares of the community; if Terence's description of the good man, as one to whom no human interest is foreign, be correct—then Dr. Virchow is the model citizen, and the model philanthropist. For instance, he is, and has been since 1859, a member of the municipal chamber, and has faithfully performed the humble duties of alderman. He is one of the lecturers before the "Berlin Mechanics' Union." He belongs to the directors of the "Union for Domestic and Popular Instruction." For a long time he was one of the managers of the "Turners" Association, and wrote two or three pamphlets on subjects connected with popular gymnastics. To enumerate all the scientific, benevolent, and other societies of which he is a member, would fill two pages. He even received the offer of a seat in the Imperial Parliament, but declined it for reasons of principle, which are worthy of explanation.

The German Empire, or its predecessor, the North German Confederation, issued from the battle of Sadowa. About this, all men in Prussia were agreed; but all men were not agreed as to the expediency or the honest possibility of a recognition of this new system by men who abhorred the policy that brought it forth. The majority of the House were in great distress. For four years they had shouted that Bismarck was leading Prussia to destruction, and he had answered with a united Fatherland. For more than four years they had struggled for German unity, and it came in a form which affronted all the instincts of their conscience. Should they condone the offenses of the past, or destroy the fair promises of the future? The answer to this question rent the Party of Progress asunder. It was an affair of personal conviction, with which no caucus would presume to meddle; and while half the Liberals accepted the compromise, the other half resolutely refused it. Professor Gneist, who had once branded the Bismarck policy with the mark of Cain, was one of the most eager, by a vote of indemnity, to wash it out again. Professor Virchow was less merciful and less confiding. He not only would not stultify himself, by voting pardon for a long and deliberate violation of the public charter, but he was also one of the little band which preserved, amid the seductions of an idle patriotism, the name and principles of the Progress party. He would not grant immunity for the policy which created the empire; he would not accept the machinery of government proposed for that empire; he would not even accept a seat in its highest legislative assembly. In this fidelity to principle, he and Jacoby stood alone. Their position may have been false in logic, and an error of statesmanship, but it was maintained at some cost to them of honor and convenience, and it is not easy to refuse them a certain measure of admiration.

Dr. Virchow is a voluminous author. In addition to the works already mentioned, he has published a small library of works, books and pamphlets, special and professional, besides hundreds of magazine articles and speeches. A list of his more important works will give a notion far from adequate of his restless activity. In 1849, he printed "The Unification Struggle in Scientific Medicine," which contained a partial exposition of his pathological theories. The so-called cellular theory was first stated at length in the volume published in 1859, under the title, "Lectures upon Cellular Pathology, as grounded upon the Physiological and Pathological Theory of Tissue." This was afterwards incorporated as the first volume of the larger work completed in 1862, which was called simply "Lectures on Pathology." In 1856, he published a collection of fugitive articles, under the title, "Contributions to Scientific Medicine;" in 1854, in connection with other eminent gentlemen, the "Hand-book of Special Pathology and Therapeutics;" in 1857, "Investigations into the Development of the Skull;" in 1862, "Four Discourses upon Life and Sickness;" in 1865, "The Theory of Trichina;" in 1861, "Gœthe as a Naturalist," etc., etc. In company with Professor von Holtzendorff, of Munich, he edits a series of popular scientific treatises, to which he himself has contributed two numbers. The articles written by him for the "Turners" and other special societies, have already been mentioned.

Dr. Virchow is a man slightly under the medium height, but of good proportions. He has a clear, strong voice, his gestures and elocution are good, and his style is throughout forcible and impressive. Although he is nominally a member of the Party of Progress, he is really an independent member, who speaks and votes from conviction, and not for or with any party.

XVIII.

Professor von Treitschke.

THIS robust and popular politician was born on the 15th of October, 1834, at Dresden, and belonged to a respectable Protestant family. He pursued his studies at the universities of Bonn, Leipsic, Tübingen, and Heidelberg. A popular *garçon* among his fellows at school, he was also a showy and brilliant student, and a favorite debater at college clubs, and elsewhere. Although a man of firm Liberal convictions, he had also an unusual moderation and maturity of view. He was then, and is now, a Conservative, with the fiery speech and ardent eloquence of a Radical—a graceful writer and a convincing speaker, but utterly free from every form of fanaticism.

On his "promotion" or graduation, he won honors in history, especially political history, and was appointed *Privat-Docent* at Leipsic, where he remained till 1863. From thence he passed to the University of Freiburg, where he became Professor. In 1866, he accepted an invitation to Kiel, and soon afterward to Heidelberg, where he succeeded the famous historian, Häusser.

The course of events which led to this order of succession was political, as well as scholastic, and in explaining that, we explain the circumstances of Treitschke's *debut* in public life. It will be recollected that after the Danish war of 1864, and the occupation of the Duchies by the united armies of Austria and Prussia, the problem arose, to find a permanent adjustment of the new relations. The Liberals perhaps regarded the embarrassment with a secret satisfaction. They had asserted that war to be as unjust and unnecessary, as it was unlawfully undertaken and cruelly conducted; and they could take a pardonable delight in the fact that the conquest left the political complications more perplexing than before. The central object of aversion, not to say hatred, was, of course, Herr von Bismarck, Prussian minister-president. These feelings were even stronger among non-Prussians, than among Prussians; for, while the latter criticised his course only as a matter of domestic politics, the former viewed it as part of a scheme for effecting German unity, by means which they abhorred. The invasion of the Duchies was regarded by the smaller States as an unwarrantable aggression on German rights.

In this state of things, the literature of the question received a sudden and remarkable addition. Heinrich von Treitschke was a Liberal, and a non-Prussian, a Saxon by birth, who had been almost driven from Leipsic because he was too liberal; and he now came forward to defend Bismarck's policy in the Duchies. His pamphlet was called "The Parties and the Duchies."* Its immediate object was to vindicate the treatment which Prince

---

* "*Die Parteien und die Herzogthümer.*"

Frederic, one of the candidates for the succession in the Duchies, had received from the two allied powers, and more particularly from Prussia, under Bismarck's directions. But this was not all. It had been said above that the Danish war was a German event, and that Bismarck's policy was so far a German question, that the position of Prussians in Germany would be determined largely by the consequences of that event. Treitschke had, therefore, a double duty. He had to justify Herr von Bismarck, not only to Prussia, but also to Germany. He had to show, not only that the occupation of the Duchies, and the expulsion of Prince Frederic, were sagacious measures in the interest of Prussia, but that, in a larger sense, the hopes of German unity lay in a strong and compact State fused around Prussia, rather than a loose Confederation, with "Particularism" everywhere triumphant. In other words, the young professor came forward as the South German champion of Prussian leadership in the distracted fatherland.

The pamphlet made a great sensation. The author was but little known, either in literary or academic circles. It was discovered that he had published, in 1856, a volume of sonnets, which were more distinguished for their patriotic than their poetical spirit. In 1859, he had written a work on Social Science,* which had but moderate success, and is now forgotten. It was also learned that some scholarly and ingenious essays, on historical and biographical subjects in two or three leading periodicals, were from his pen. After the appearance of his pamphlet in defense of Bismarck, however, the country recognized in him a literary

---

* "*Die Gesellschaftswissenschaft.*"

and a political talent of the first order ; and the files of the periodical literature were eagerly searched, with the result above described. A demand for their republication became felt, and was satisfied. The historical and critical essays, a biographical sketch of Wagenheim, and the famous pamphlet, were collected in a single volume,* and given out to the world. From that time, his literary position, at least, was assured.

In the *Grenzboten*, the effect produced by Treitschke's pamphlet is graphically described.

"'The effect,' says a writer, in the periodical to which Treitschke himself contributed, "was powerful. The pedants and hucksters of history raged over this boldness of view and frankness of speech ; many a professional teacher of history shook continually his shaggy head. The Liberal Philistines in the North, and still more in the South, growled or howled anger and wrath against the renegade, who had so little respect for the phrases of Liberalism. And, although in many circles, Treitschke's historical assertions supplied a defect in political reflection and political education, his tone was still held to be too passionate, too vivacious, too positive and dogmatic. Unreserved applause Treitschke received, at first, only from a few. But the more he was read, the more clearly there was recognized, in his spirited language, concise historical truth ; so much the more general became the conviction that he united a warm patriotic feeling with a remarkably clear and deep insight into the more recent German history. At first, the fresh aphorisms of the young publicist

---

* "*Historische und Politische Aufsätze.*"

may easily have passed for political fancies, for one-sided theories. With closer and deeper study, one recognized a basis of historical study, from which political judgments had securely built themselves up. In scientific circles, also, the recognition and appreciation of Treitschke began to rise." *

His pamphlet, indeed, did not rest unanswered. It called forth a multitude of replies, which, as is commonly the case, wanted the freshness, and failed to win the celebrity of the original work. But the Prussian government did not forget its bold champion. After the war of 1866 and the expulsion of Austria from the Duchies, the University of Kiel became a Prussian institution, and Treitschke joined its faculty as professor of history.

The significance of Treitschke's appointment to Heidelberg, on the death of Häusser, lay in the opposite political tendencies of the two men. Häusser was a veteran in German academic circles, and in German historical literature, and enjoyed a great and deserved authority in the North and in the South. But he was one of the most strenuous opponents of Prussia. One of the last occasions on which his pen was employed, was devoted to a severe and vigorous arraignment of Bismarck, for the Danish war; and his last injunction to his countrymen was to resist the aggressions of Prussian statesmanship. He died, and the most conspicuous defender of Bismarck and Prussia became his successor at Heidelberg.

Treitschke's religious views have been the subject of much dispute. He was accused of being, and doubtless is,

---

* *Die Grenzboten*, 1872, No. 15, page 44.

a Rationalist, but he once gave so eloquent a statement of his respect for piety and the pious, that it deserves to be reproduced. He blamed, he said, the presumption of learning, which looked down superciliously upon the modest faith of the unlearned. "Never," continued he, "can the most intense scientific conviction replace in any man the blessings of belief! Before the eternal problems of life, before the questions which most deeply torture and agitate the soul, the scholar is as helpless as the peasant. From such questions only a mine of unfruitful resignation leads away—or the force of faith, the conviction conquered in severe trials of the soul, that the inconceivable is the all-certain, that God is just, and his dispositions wise. I am still the free-thinker that I was fourteen years ago, when I wrote the article on freedom. I hold to-day that not *what*, but *how* we believe, determines the moral dignity of manhood. But during this fruitful period, the religious feeling in me is becoming stronger. I have gratefully seen the work of Providence in the fortunes of my country, as well as my own house, and I feel more keenly than heretofore the need of bowing humbly before God. Through the intellectual conflicts of the present, an incurable breach has been made in our people. This condition is far too unnatural to be perpetuated in a conscientious nation. Every one, without exception, is poorer in heart when he stifles the religious feeling within him."* The reader will be able to say whether religion is in much danger from a man who can write such a passage as this!

---

* "*Sendschreiben an Gustav Schmoller.*"

In 1871, Professor von Treitschke became a member of the Imperial Parliament. Although his entrance upon a legislative career was greeted by many with enthusiasm, and by all with interest, his success was impaired by an unfortunate physical infirmity—deafness. He cannot follow the course of debate, he cannot even understand the whispers of his immediate neighbors. One of these, however, Dr. Wehrenpfennig, renders him a touching and graceful service. Sitting patiently by his friend's side, he writes rapidly, with a pencil, while Treitschke eagerly reads, the points made or raised during the discussion, the causes of laughter or tumult, and from time to time the progress and conditions of pending measures. These hints are, indeed, the conditions of Treitschke's intelligent interest in parliamentary work, but not alone the texts for his speeches. These are rather the philosophic harangues of a patriot, than the disputatious pleas of a politician. It would be unjust to call them essays, spoken from the tribune, instead of published in the *Preussische Jahrbücher*. They are always practical and pertinent, real contributions to the question at issue, incisive in form and impassioned in tone, thoughtful without being dull, and clear without being shallow ; and if they read better than they sound, the orator, and not the debater, is at fault. Deaf men are notoriously, and for obvious reasons, poor speakers. With all admiration for his great literary talents, for the elevated purity of his character, and for the romantic devotion with which he pursues his difficult task, I am compelled to say that Treitschke is one of the most outrageous speakers who ever addressed an audience. He has no control over his voice, his intonation, or his utterance. He mumbles, and roars, and shrieks ;

he brandishes his arms and shakes his fists; he pounds with hands and feet; and during all these physical contortions, never interrupts the foaming torrent of his words. His manner is more that of a fanatic, or a madman, than of a moderate and somewhat Conservative professor. Edmund Burke said of a certain pamphleteer of the French Revolution, that he railed against monks in the spirit of a monk. In the same way, it may be said of Treitschke's manner, though not of his matter, that he declaims against Socialism with the violence of a *pétroleur*. In one respect his deafness is a blessing. He does not hear the angry interruptions—now from the benches of the Ultramontanes, now from the corner where sit the Socialists—but tears along with his philippic, undisturbed, to the end. Sometimes his faithful friend, Wehrenpfennig reaches up to him a slip of paper with an important hint, but the furious orator notices it no more than a fly on his desk.

In spite of all this, the reader may be not unprepared to believe that Professor Treitschke is one of the most successful speakers in the House. No other member is heard with more respect, or more interest. When he mounts the tribune, his brother deputies, from all parts of the House, and of every political party, gather hurriedly around him in order that they may catch every word of his remarkable speeches. The chairman leans eagerly over his table to listen; Bismarck lays down his long pencil and draws near the scene of interest. Even the cynical Windthorst sometimes forgets to sneer. The nervous invective and impetuous rhetoric have a strange fascination for the hearers; and when Treitschke retires to his seat the House visibly arouses, as if it had been under the spell of some violent but refreshing storm. The worthy citizen who reads such a discourse the next day in his newspaper, will admire its literary and philosophical beauties. But the severe critic in the gallery, who may be familiar with the best oratory of France, and England, and America; who may have heard a Jules Favre, or a Wendell Phillips, will be at a loss to explain the enthusiasm shown toward such a speaker; a speaker who has neither grace of manner, nor of elocution, nor any of the prescribed virtues of an orator, except an intense earnestness, which is revealed in a turgid, furious and unintelligible declamation.

On the other hand, the literary style of Treitschke, as shown in his published writings, is of the very highest order. The critic, who has already been quoted, says justly that he "is a master of the essay form. Previously little known by us Germans, little used, and highly valued, the historical essay has begun within the last two decades to play a great *rôle*. It offers to him who knows how to manage it, many advantages. An author, who has undertaken to treat a given historical subject, can allow his own views greater license in an essay, than in an elaborate book. It is permitted to him to take up only the sides which more particularly attract him, or on which he can throw special light. * * * He who considers together the various works of Treitschke, will be able to make the distinction clear. He will see how the studies of this writer include and encompass the entire national life of our century, with all its interests of the most different kinds. And he will observe even while his eye is upon the work as a whole, how carefully Treitschke has concentrated his labor upon certain leading subjects, how he has assigned to himself, in single essays, the special and thorough treatment of selected topics. We may almost say that the bases of a history of the civilized peoples of the nineteenth century are to be found in these dissertations. The author nowhere betrays an intention to undertake such a history. In each essay he treats the subject in a way that easily reveals the philosophical completeness of his studies, but leaves to each the unimpaired freedom of its own nature. * * * And the works of the professor, however much they may seem to be the product of party spirit, however elegant their outward form, are the results of deep, exhaustive, real scientific studies."*

Treitschke is joint editor, with Dr. Wehrenpfennig, of the *Preussische Jahrbücher*, one of the most considerable periodicals of Germany. It is in this that all of his later essays have first appeared, and it is his name which, more than any other element, contributes to its success. The Germans are not great readers of periodical literature. A newspaper of the better class, which reaches a circulation of ten thousand copies, daily, is already a great triumph. The leading literary weekly, which corresponds to the weekly reviews of England and America, is exceptionally prosperous with a regular issue of seven thousand, and a monthly review, which, within a year, has won about ten thousand subscribers, is justly regarded as a phenomenal success. It is unnecessary here to inquire into the causes of this fact. But one circumstance, which long impaired the circulation of the more serious periodicals, was the fatuous timidity with which they confined themselves to

---

* *Grenzboten*, 1872, No. 15, pp. 48, 49.

abstract or neutral subjects, and evaded the fresh living issues of the hour. Writers who had a political question to discuss, or a concrete political proposition of any sort to maintain, were obliged to print a pamphlet at their own risk, and their own cost. The magazines had, and in a measure still have, no hospitality for them. And on the other hand, men who wished to bring their political reading down to topics and controversies less remote than the Roman Republic, were forced to buy a library of *brochures*, or satisfy themselves with the more hasty and superficial articles of the daily press.

Of this state of things Professor Treitschke has been one of the most successful reformers. It would be inexact to say that he is the founder of the critical essay in Germany; but he has given it greater power and popularity, and he has opened to it one entirely new class of subjects. He has dignified and exalted the issues of practical politics, by applying to them, in elaborate essays, all the literary graces of a finished writer, the ample resources of a Liberal and accomplished scholar, and the critical analysis of a philosophic mind. He has taught his countrymen that the problems of the present are of eternal importance, and that the thinker, not the empiric, must find the solution. His success is shown in the improved character of German serials. Although they still want the boldness and independence that our prejudices exact, they nevertheless exhibit a growing freshness and spirit, which the real friend of Germany must observe with pleasure. The essays of Treitschke would seem to be taken as models, even by writers who could not attain, and do not aspire, to their excellence.

Professor Treitschke does not always proclaim in the titles of his essays their relations to actual issues. He has, on the contrary, the valuable art of insinuating his theories upon the reader, of enforcing them in the form of inference and deduction, and thereby retaining to the end the charmed attention of pedants, who abhor a concrete discussion. Sometimes, indeed, the subject is fearlessly announced, as in the article on "Union or Confederation,"* or in the one upon the question of two Chambers in the Prussian Parliament.† More commonly, however, he gave greater breadth and dignity to his political lessons by founding them upon some general discussions in history, or illustrating them from certain characters, which are to be imitated or abhorred. Thus his sketch of Wagenheim was merely a text on which he hung a masterly exposure of German "Particularism," that perverse and demoralizing element in the politics of the fatherland. The same is true of his different articles on Italian, French and English political history. From each of these subjects there is extracted some moral or lesson, for particular application to the current necessities of Prussian or German society.

It required no small amount of courage for Professor Treitschke to take a chair in history, at the University of Berlin. That institution already counted in that branch some of the most illustrious scholars of the present day; such men as Curtius in Greek, and Mommsen in Roman history, Droysen, in modern German history, and

---

* "*Einheitsstaat oder Bundesstaat.*"
† "*Der Preussische Landtag und das Zweikammersystem.*"

the name, if no longer the active participation, of the veteran Ranke. Droysen, in particular, is a scholar who, devoting himself to the same general class of subjects as Treitschke, has many of the same literary and intellectual characteristics. He has a vivacious style and a clear delivery; his Life of York, and other works, have given him deserved authority; and he is a favorite lecturer with the younger students. Treitschke's subjects are selected from the same general period, but his method of treatment is less historical, less concrete; in a word, less "objective" and more abstract or speculative. He has struck out for himself a new path and followed it with brilliant success. He really teaches the political art in the light of political history. He holds a position midway between jurists who expound the positive ordinances of civil government, and historians who relate events in lifeless chronological order. Already, his lecture room is one of the most popular in the institution. His style and manner here are less objectionable than on the floor of Parliament. The general faults of his delivery, especially such as are inseparable from his deafness, are never wholly conquered; but in the clear air of scholastic work, they are less prominent, less extravagantly obtrusive, than amid the passions and excitements of the legislative hall. He has the faculty, so dear to teachers, of inspiring his pupils with enthusiasm, as well as confidence.

It is stated, or rumored, that Treitschke will not always confine his historical productions to the modest form of essays, but that a great work may, some day, be expected from his pen. This is described as a history of the nineteenth century in Germany. The *Grenzboten* affirms positively that he has long been engaged in collecting and arranging the materials for such a work, but vouchsafes no opinion as to the date of its appearance. The period is one which Treitschke is specially qualified to treat, and this gives the report a certain probability. There is, indeed, every reason to expect frequent and even more important works from this capable writer; and, in his academic career, steady progress and repeated triumphs undoubtedly await him. That the same may be predicated of his political career, is less certain. An ingenious critic, much esteemed for the freshness and elegance of his style,— a debater admired, with all his defects, for the chivalric impetuosity of his manner,—he wants many of the qualities and most of the conditions of a statesman. This is the misfortune of Prussia, but it is a misfortune which has its sources in two centuries of the national history.

It remains to add that, Professor Treitschke, if a genius, is in appearance an unkempt genius. He is a large, massive man, with a heavy black beard, and a very marked oriental complexion. His gait, though rapid, is clumsy and erratic; and in all his movements he impresses as one who has an excess of nervous force. If his large head suggests the man of brain and thought, the broad shoulders and ample chest supply the physical conditions of hard study and intense endurance. But for his unfortunate deafness, he might be taken as a model of that even development of the corporeal and the spiritual, that mutual adaptation of mind and body, of which a Latin phrase gives the happy and favorite expression.

XIX.

Professor von Sybel.

THE list of German politicians, who have also a reputation as scholars and teachers, may fitly be closed with Profsssor von Sybel. But it is far from being exhausted. We might add a score or two of names but little less important. In the *Reichstag*, for instance, there now sit, or have recently sat, such men as Dr. Baumgarten, the famous Liberal theologian, now professor at Rostock; Dr. Ewald, the great Hebraist, recently deceased; Professor Beseler, a jurist in the Berlin University; Dr. Buss, professor at Freiburg; Professor Hänel, of Kiel; Hinschius, the great authority at canon law; Marquardsen, of Erlangen; Merkle, professor at the Lyceum at Dillingen; Robert von Mohl, the publicist, recently dead; Oncken, of Geissen; Schmidt, of Jena; von Schulte, of Bonn; Dr. Tellkampf, of Breslau; besides a number of lesser personages. To these might be added several other scholars, who are members only of the Prussian, or other separate Legislatures. The deputies are paid in the *Reichstag* nothing, in the local parliaments very little; and the conditions of legislative work here are such that very few of these learned men can hope, thereby, to add much to their scholastic reputations. That they are willing to leave their books and papers for the service of the State, and that the electors are willing to elect them over the professional politicians, is equally creditable to both parties. It may be true, as has been pretended, that German scholarship will suffer from this circumstance. That German politics, however, are elevated, and dignified, and purified, seems to me beyond dispute.

It must be admitted, however, that not even the strictest line of distinction would exclude from active political work a student and professor of political history, and such a man is Heinrich von Sybel. He was born on the 2d of December, 1817, at Düsseldorf. After his preparatory and university studies, he came to Berlin, and entered the so-called "Historical Seminary," which was under the direction of Leopold von Ranke, and enjoyed the benefits of his great authority. Here he remained four years, from 1834 to 1838. His first work was published in 1841, on his return to Düsseldorf, and was a "History of the First Crusade." Its object was to prove that Peter the Hermit was not the originator, and Godfrey of Bouillon not the leader of that expedition. A controversial rather than a historical work, it had interest chiefly for scholars. The product of a young man, it was, also, in tone and treatment, a product of the school from which he came. Dr. von Ranke was very successful in impressing not only his method, but also his general views and principles upon his young admirers, and the "school" called after him, is an important literary phenomenon in Germany. Von Sybel was less under the influence of the master than some of his colleagues, and, in succeeding works, has almost wholly emancipated himself.

This book on the Crusades, and the reputation that he won under Ranke, led to von Sybel's appointment at Bonn, where he became adjunct professor in 1844. One year later, he was invited to Marburg, as regular professor. His entry into political life occurred soon afterwards. The university chose him, as its representative, in 1847, to the Assembly of the Hessian Estates. He was also one of the Hessian delegates to the German Parliament at Erfurt. In both these assemblies von Sybel was classed as a Constitutional Conservative, a strong friend of German unity, but an enemy of all violent measures.

It was also at this epoch, that von Sybel's literary reputation may be said to have begun. His "History of the French Revolution."* appeared in three volumes, during the years 1853-57, and was at once successful. It discarded the graphic and picturesque style of which Johann von Müller and Frederic von Raumer were the best representatives, and affected rather the grave, reflective, analytic manner of Ranke. It was critical, concise, judicial, never discursive for the sake of his art, and it seldom wandered from the subject to paint a character or a scene. But it is not heavy, and does not repel the ordinary reader. It has already passed through three German editions, the last in 1866, and has been translated into English, French, and most European tongues.

Geschichte der Revolutionszeit in Frankreich.

One of the immediate results of the book was the author's invitation to the University of Munich, a summons which he accepted. In this delightful resort of the Muses, he seems to have enjoyed, at once, the honors of a scholar, the facilities of a student, and the opportunities of a teacher. The King, Maximilian II., himself a scho'ar, was a judicious patron of art, and literature, and science; besides making von Sybel president of the so-called Royal Historical Commission, encouraged the organization of the Historical Seminary, which von Sybel had so much at heart, and entrusted him with many confidential State charges. If the professor had cared only for academic honors and a life of elegant literary retirement, he might have remained at Munich till this day. It is more probable, however, that the old feelings of a Prussian never forsook him, and that in the midst of the comforts and facilities, which he enjoyed at that place, the charms of the broader political life in his native State proved too strong for him. Accordingly, when, in 1861, an opportunity to return to Bonn was opened, he hastened to improve it.

His return to political life, or rather, for Prussia, his entry upon political life followed in 1862, at the earliest legal moment. It happened to coincide pretty nearly with the appointment of Bismarck·as Minister President. In view of the strenuous opposition which he made to the earlier policy of that ministry, Wolfgang Menzel accuses him of ingratitude, which is inexact, for, as above stated, he was called to Bonn nearly a year before Bismarck took office, and therefore, owed his government no thanks. It was, perhaps, magnanimous in the government not to dismiss him as soon as his dangerous revolutionary sentiments were discovered. In those days, a Liberal could not be too grateful for a little. But the fact of his opposition to the unconstitutional measures of the ministry, is, to-day, one of the things of which Professor von Sybel is not least proud.

At the very outset of his parliamentary career, Professor von Sybel was a leading actor in a well-known scene. Although, in form, it was only a personal altercation between him and the Minister of War, Count von Roon, it involved, in fact, a question of principle, of parliamentary law, which, to this day, has not been finally settled. One of the most characteristic incidents of the long struggle between Bismarck's Ministry and the House of Deputies, it well deserves to be explained in this place. It has already been briefly mentioned.

It was on the 11th of May, 1863. The House had just been convened after a long recess, and the usual angry and boisterous scenes had been renewed. General von Roon had made an appeal to the patriotism of the House, in behalf of the army reform, when von Sybel replied scornfully, that the War Minister had no right to speak of patriotism. He had done more than any other to alter the conditions of public law in Prusssia. If, for the first time in his career, he wished to do a patriotic thing, let him retire from the ministry. The War Minister answered: "When such personal remarks are made against a member of the ministry, it is an unjustifiable aggression." The President of the House interrupted the minister, and by means of his bell, supported by the clamors of the majority, forced him to silence. Then he explained: "The

War Minister had no right to call the remark of Professor von Sybel an unjustifiable aggression. It belonged only to him, the president, to censure those remarks, if he found them censurable. He had not done that, however, for Herr von Sybel was fully within his rights." The War Minister protested against the violence of the House, whereupon new tumult followed. Finally, the president was forced to suspend the sitting, and, as is usual in such cases, he reached out for a hat to cover himself, but, as the hat happened not to be his own, but another much too large for him, it fell down over his ears, to the great amusement of the deputies. The tragedy was nearly converted into a comedy.

But this was not the end of the matter. The government denied absolutely the disciplinary power of the President of the House over the ministers, and declared that they would attend no more sessions until their exemption from the restraints of parliamentary law was expressly acknowledged. This was, of course, impossible. The House replied with an address to the King, which not only justified the conduct of its president, but called for the immediate dismissal of the ministers. The King replied, on the 26th of the month, with an autograph letter, not countersigned by a single minister. An extract or two from this document will give an interesting illustration of the royal prerogative, as it was understood by his majesty, and will show the almost impossible gulf which separated him from the deputies. "Prussia's Kings," he wrote, "live in and with their people, and have a clear eye and a warm heart for the real needs of the country. About the proceedings in the session of May 11th, I was accurately and faithfully informed. The fact is clear, that the chairman not only interrupted one of my ministers, and forced him to silence, but also prevented him, by a sudden adjournment, from subsequently speaking. This act can only be interpreted on the theory that it was an application of the disciplinary power of the president." Such a claim his majesty repelled, and after some further observations, concluded: "My ministers possess my confidence, their official acts had my approval, and I am grateful to them that they feel the importance of opposing the unconstitutional usurpation of the House of Deputies."

This was the royal view of constitutional government in Prussia, in the year 1863. It is not a little to the credit of a man like von Sybel, whose position at Bonn depended on the favor of the government, that he was willing, publicly and persistently, to oppose that view.

After this incident, the House was dissolved by the government, and new elections were ordered for the Autumn of the same year. They resulted, as usual, in strong Liberal majorities. Professor von Sybel was also re-elected for the district of Crefeld. In the Spring of the next year, 1864, a disease of his eyes, which had long troubled him, became too serious for longer participation in active legislative work, and he was obliged to resign.

Since the appearance of his French History, in part at Bonn, in part at Marburg, and in part at Munich, he has published a number of less pretentious historical treatises, which deserve to be mentioned. I shall simply give their titles in English: "The Origin of German Monarchy," 1845; "The Spuriousness of the so-called Sacred Robe at Trèves," 1845; "The Uprising of Europe against

Napoleon I," 1860; "Prince Eugene of Savoy," 1861; "The German Nation and the Empire," 1863; and a collection called "Minor Historical Writings," 1863.

In the year 1867, immediately after the war with Austria, von Sybel returned to political life. The district Lennep-Mettmann sent him to the so-called *Constituent Reichstag*, which was summoned by Prussia to lay the foundations of the North German Confederation, and to confirm on an imposing scale the truce concluded between the majority and the government. Von Sybel was, as we have seen in 1863, one of the most resolute opponents of Bismarck's policy. In 1867, he was not one of the irreconcilables. He joined the National Liberals and voted steadily, though not slavishly with them; and his profound historical knowledge gave him peculiar authority in the reconstruction of Germany. He did not accept an election to the Legislative Parliament. His third term of political service ended here.

His fourth and present term began with the existing *Landtag* of Prussia, which was elected in 1874. Professor von Sybel is the delegate of a district near Magdeburg. When he took his seat, the ecclesiastical conflict had been in progress three years, and though the spirit of the Catholics was not broken, and a number of measures were still threatened, the freshness of the subject had departed, and the people were becoming weary of it. Even Professor von Sybel had been active with his pen. From his retreat, at Bonn, which is a semi-Catholic university, he had already sent out a number of pamphlets in which the pretensions of the Church were exposed, and the rights of the State vindicated with the resources of an historical scholar, and the vigor of an earnest patriot. These had been accompanied, also, by public discourses, articles in the leading periodicals, and, above all, by his contributions to the *Historische Zeitschrift*, of which he was and remains the editor. An account of these and other papers will be given in another place.

Two leading anti-clerical measures have, however, been introduced since von Sybel's return to the House; and, in the debates which preceded their adoption, he was one of the most frequent and successful speakers. The measures were: first, to dissolve and abolish all Catholic religious orders and congregations, except purely benevolent ones; and, second, to suspend all State contributions for the support of the Roman Catholic worship. These were, by far, the most sweeping bills in the long course of ecclesiastical legislation. In Professor von Sybel the Ultramontanes found an antagonist of a new order. Most of the Liberal speakers were either learned doctors without the experience and method of politics, or practical politicians without the necessary special training for the subject; but the new member was at once a scholar and a man of the world, a debater who could meet the foe on the field of ecclesiastical law, or the field of secular politics.

In the present month, March, 1876, an additional or supplementary bill was presented. It regulates, or rather provides for the control by the State, of the estates and funds of such Catholic dioceses, as may be without their episcopal head. There are several such in Prussia, made vacant by the removal of the bishops, under the operation of the State laws, and kept vacant by the refusal of the Pope to appoint successors. The pending bill is, therefore, only a logical consequence of previous legislation.

It is, however, a singular feature of these clerical debates, that they are never special, but general. They do not turn upon the merits or defects of the particular measure before the House, but upon the general issues involved in the quarrel between Church and State. This will be illustrated in the following extract from the speech of Professor von Sybel, on the 7th of March. I give it with all the interruptions and altercations, as a picture of the ecclesiastical contest.

"I am glad to be able to state," said Professor Sybel, "that I entirely agree with some sentiments of the honorable gentleman who preceded me. The first point of agreement is, that this bill will be accepted by the House. Next, that this bill, as well as that of last year about the Parish Funds, has nothing to do with the inner affairs of the Church. From this standpoint all the Falk laws were issued, and they have the one aim, to draw the line between Church and State, in a healthy and normal manner, and to re-establish in Prussia the inalienable rights of the State, which, through a narrow and false policy, had fallen into neglect. The honorable deputy sighs: 'Since the beginning of this contest, we Roman Catholics have not been treated as citizens of the State, but as aliens.' This *pluralis majestatis*, 'we Roman Catholics,' is with you a fluent figure of speech. You always act as if there were no Roman Catholics in the country, except you and your friends. Yet, Dr. Falk, during his travels through the Rhenish towns, was able to see very clearly how many Roman Catholics there are, who are not at all of your opinion ('Oh!' in the center); who do not consider themselves aliens, and are not treated as such. The question might be pertinent with a great many of your party: Are they, in any sense, still children of the State? Do they still consider themselves subjects of the Prussian Crown? Are they not simply subjects of his Papal Holiness, and no one else? ('Oh!' and laughter in the center.) This fact runs parallel with a set of principles which we have often heard expressed by you. So much is certain, that if you answer my question with a dry, 'No'; if you declare 'No, we are only subjects of the Pope in ecclesiastical matters, in other matters we are not' (*Herr Reichensperger:* 'Undoubtedly!'), then you would certainly receive from Rome a very prompt rectification. (Merriment.) Then read the semi-official organ of the Roman Curia, the *Voce della Verità*. You have praised, in all your organs, the latest literary production of the Reichensperger Muse, this so-called 'Word for Peace.' Whoever has read that interesting little book, feels convinced that all these peaceful proposals amount solely to the subjection of the State under the Church. Yet, it is announced in form and title as a 'Word for Peace!' Now notice how the *Voce della Verità* expresses itself upon this work for peace, and the Reichensperger pamphlet. Just notice how, here from high places, the author is being lectured. (Laughter from the left.) Read how he is enjoined, for the future, to correct his conceptions of Prussian relations, and not to cherish the illusion that there could ever exist a Hohenzollern who was not a born enemy of the Romish Church. ('Hear!' from the left.) Or read the *Civiltà Cattolica*, this organ established by his Holiness himself, and always controlled by him. (Cry: 'That is not true.') That is certainly true, the official documents have been published. In the October number of last year you can read the simple sentences: 'Whoever hears the Pope, hears God. We must not only obey him unconditionally in act, but also in thought and will.' There is no reference to any kind of difference between religious and civil actions. This arch-sovereign upholds his claims to his mediæval sovereignty to-day, as at all times. If the honorable gentleman who has just spoken is right, that through the law valid until now, Archbishop Förster was absolutely authorized to carry off 900,000 marks across the frontier, then, indeed, I do not know of a more forcible argument for the necessity of changing this legalized condition of things. ('Very true!') I perfectly agree with Herr Reichensperger, that the Ministers Räumer and Müller were not only passive lookers-on at the growth of this system, which at last, in our time, forced the State into defense, but they also carried eagerly, with their own hands, bricks for the edifice of ecclesiastical sovereignty. We regret this from the depth of our heart, for, without such conduct on the part of the government of that time, there would, at present, have been no occasion for any *Kulturkampf* (ecclesiastical contest). But the more mistakes that were made on all sides, at those times, the more pressing is the duty to-day, after the consequences have so plainly come to light, at last, to put a stop to it, and, in the interest of the nation and of the State, to return to the former condition and earlier system."

Professor von Sybel is an industrious pamphleteer. I have a number of his brochures before me, and a long list of others which have appeared within the past few years. Some of them are on literary or abstract questions; one or two are historical dissertations, of more or less permanent value; and some are on the political issues of the day. Under the first class, for instance, must be named the following: "On the Laws of Historical Knowledge," "The German and Foreign Universities," "On the Emancipation of Women," "The Founding of the University of Bonn," and "At the Monument to Stein." The second will include: "On the Development of Absolute Monarchy in Prussia," "Prussia and Rhineland," and "Napoleon III." This latter pamphlet was made up of two lectures delivered at Cologne, in the year 1873, and it was widely read and criticised at the time of its appearance. Finally the third class, or controversial writings, comprise, among others, the following: "The New Germany, and France, Letter to M. Forçade, in Paris," "What we can learn from France," and "The Doctrines of Socialism and Communism." None of these productions are popular in style and treatment, but they have obtained, most of them, a wide circulation.

About a year since, Professor von Sybel was appointed

keeper of the Archives of Prussia. This is one of the most confidential and responsible positions which a man of letters can hold, under the Prussian or any other government of Europe, and the distinction is, of course, highly prized. It necessitated the resignation of the professorship at Bonn, and the professor's removal to Berlin. Since he has held the position, he has not only made many useful practical reforms, but he has also agitated one literary, or rather historical scheme of the greatest importance. This is nothing less than the publication of the political correspondence of Frederic the Great. This has lain buried for years among the State papers, and it is now proposed to publish it to the world. The arrangement of the work would probably be under the general supervision of Professor von Sybel. The cost of the undertaking—no slight sum, in view of the thirty or more volumes which the correspondence would fill—has been accepted by the Berlin Academy of Sciences, a body whose enlightened labors have already placed the learned world under great obligations.

THE END.